Human Resource Management in
Today's Academic Library

Recent Titles in
The Libraries Unlimited Library Management Collection
Formerly entitled Greenwood Library Management Collection

Human Resource Management in Today's Academic Library

Meeting Challenges and Creating Opportunities

Edited by
Janice Simmons-Welburn and Beth McNeil

Libraries Unlimited Library Management Collection
Gerard McCabe, Series Adviser

LIBRARIES
UNLIMITED
A Member of the Greenwood Publishing Group

Westport, Connecticut • London

British Library Cataloguing in Publication Data is available.

ISBN: 0-313-32076-4
ISSN: 0894-2986

First published in 2004.

Libraries Unlimited, 88 Post Road West, Westport, CT 06881
A Member of the Greenwood Publishing Group, Inc.
www.lu.com

Printed in the United States of America

∞™

The paper used in this book complies with the
Permanent Paper Standard issued by the National
Information Standards Organization (Z39.48–1984).

10 9 8 7 6 5 4 3 2 1

Contents

Acknowledgments

We would like to thank our contributors for agreeing to be a part of this effort. We would also like to thank Paul Anderson, Nancy Baker, Stella Bentley, Barbara Dewey, Joan Giesecke, Carla Stoffle, and Lance Query for their willingness to share their thoughts on recruitment, leadership, and diversity issues in the context of human resources management as they appear in the final chapter, "Conversations with Our Leaders."

Finally, a special thanks to William and David for their ongoing support and insights.

Introduction

Janice Simmons-Wellburn

From Personnel to Human Resources

There has been a substantial growth in the literature on human resources management in libraries since the 1989 publication of the second edition of Sheila Creth and Frederick Duda's collection of essays, *Personnel Administration in Libraries*. At that time the editors of that volume observed the growth in library personnel management since the early 1970s. They reflected upon the "broad range of complex functions" assumed by library personnel officers, which entailed the administration of contract negotiations, interpretation of a myriad of legal questions, and management of an array of problems associated with compensation, benefits, staff training, and development. Creth and Duda also chronicled the emergence of new questions about "how work is accomplished" in libraries and ensuing challenges to the organization and management of personnel activities.

Since the appearance of their work, the concept of human resource management has evolved in academic libraries. The term "Human Resources" has been widely adopted by corporations in full recognition of changing legal requirements, ethical issues, and societal and cultural expectations of the work environment, which indeed broadened the role of personnel and made it far more integral to strategic directions than it had been in the first half of the twentieth century. Creth and Duda clearly predicted the expansion of personnel from paper and records management to a key component of organizational strategy. In the context of colleges and universities, academic libraries provide campus leadership in addressing various aspects of personnel related policies and methods in areas of recruitment, diversity, and performance evaluation.

Maurice B. Line and Margaret Kinnell have observed: "Human resource departments and functions in organizations have changed in recent years in response to the recognition that people are a unique resource" (1993, 317–18). Throughout the 1990s, an increasing number of practitioners and educators in library and information science forged a broader definition of human resource management as applied to libraries, one that included greater attention to the diversity of staffs, work-life issues and assisting employees in their career development, and issues of managerial ethics. This is reflected in several important works published since 1990, including Richard Rubin's *Human Resource Management in Libraries, Managing Human Resources in Research Libraries*, a special issue of *Library Trends* edited by Anne Woodsworth and Ellen Detlefsen, Line and Kinnell's comprehensive essay, "Human Resource Management in Library and Information Services," published in the *Annual Review of Information Science and Technology*, and David A. Baldwin's *The Academic Librarian's Human Resources Handbook.*

In *Competitive Advantage through People,* Jeffrey Pfeffer suggested that in most organizations the traditional role of human resource management has been weak and peripheral to the core of the organization. He concluded:

> The simple question to ask about the human resource function is this: Is it adding value, is it solving problems, is it serving the organization's strategic business needs? If the answer is no, then perhaps management would be well advised to turn its denizens loose on the competition to do their damage elsewhere. If the answer is yes, then the function can serve as an important partner in making changes designed to help the organization achieve greater productivity and performance. In any case, the smart general manager will make sure he or she knows what the situation is and whether human resources will be an ally or an obstacle to change. (1994, 251)

The challenge, then, for academic library human resource managers in the first decade of the twenty-first century is to establish a human resources function that is affirming and highly relevant to the core of the library and to its strategic direction. This work extends previous efforts to analyze trends and issues in personnel and human resource management in academic libraries by assembling a group of essays that cover many of the major themes from this dimension of management and organizational studies of academic libraries. It is not meant to be exhaustive; rather, it is designed to shape discussions and provide practical guidance to academic librarians. The audience for this discussion is not limited to working personnel and human resources administrators in libraries. Our intent is to reach staff across the organization, from newly hired employees to senior level staff and administrators.

The first two chapters provide a context for thinking about human resource management in academic organizations. William Welburn provides a broad overview of the higher educational milieu, arguing for careful consideration of the differences between colleges and universities caused not only by characteristics but also by environments and cultures and the impact these differences have on the administration of human resources. Turning to the nexus between the demographics of the workplace and the broader society, Janice Simmons-Welburn considers various dimensions of the impact of diversity on HR. Stanley Wilder's well-publicized analysis of the impact of demographic trends on the academic library workforce is reprinted in this volume as a way of underscoring the impact not only of demographics but also changing job definitions and requirements, particularly as they affect academic research libraries.

The chapters by Laine Stambaugh, Luisa Paster, Julie Brewer, Beth McNeil, Lila Fredenburg, and Teri Switzer all supply readers with new insights and strategies on topics that are at the heart of human resources. Stambaugh examines issues pertaining to the recruitment and selection of professionals in our libraries as well as offering strategies for success. Recruiting and attracting new librarians to our profession became the topic of much discussion in the 1990s. Once we have been successful in our efforts to recruit the best and brightest, the issues of training and development become paramount. The necessity for staff development has increased as a means for enhancing organizational effectiveness. Luisa Paster draws on her experience as a Staff Development Librarian when discussing the current issues in this area. Not only is it important to address staff needs as they pertain to their particular jobs or areas of responsibilities. Work and an employee's personal life are intertwined. Employees and employers are challenged to find a balance between the two.

In recent years human resources managers have been finding themselves working with an array of federal mandates such as the American with Disabilities Act and the Family Medical Leave Act, which are intended to ensure productivity of staff. These mandates include flexible work arrangements, child care, elder care, and other employee assistance programs. Julie Brewer's chapter explores these issues more closely. There are many factors that affect an organization's approach to compensation. In addition, compensation packages have a tremendous impact on an organization's ability to compete and recruit for key positions. Beth McNeil provides a review of the issue of performance appraisals. Critical to her discussion is the link she establishes between the performance review process and the importance of career development and rewards processes in academic libraries.

Lila Fredenburg supplies the reader with a comprehensive overview of issues in labor relations as related to the world of academic libraries. Her work is especially timely in the consideration she gives to the impact of students on the labor movement, both in the support they give other unions and in their efforts to unionize and how that has impacted the relationship between libraries and student workers. Teri Switzer gives an extensive overview of benefits. She has included in her discussion strategies for higher salaries, medical benefits, retirement plans, and nonfinancial benefits.

Under the rubric of leadership, Sheila Creth and Mark Winston (chapters 10 and 12) discuss the changing role of library administrators as well as the role that graduate education can play in advancing professional knowledge of human resources issues. I offer a critique of current thinking and research on shifts in the nature of work in academic libraries in light of the influences of technology, changing organizational structures, and current thinking about continuous learning (chapter 11). Too little has been written about the role of ethics in library human resource management, and Welburn examines several recent studies conducted in different organizations in the United States and Europe in relation to earlier work by sociologist Emile Durkheim.

This volume concludes with "Conversations with Our Leaders," a roundtable discussion about human resources and academic libraries conducted with a group of veteran academic library administrators whose individual contributions are prominent in the literature of our profession.

References

Line, Maurice B., and Margaret Kinnel. 1993. "Human Resource Management in Library and Information Services." *Annual Review of Information Science and Technology* 28: 317–59.

Pfeffer, Jeffrey. 1994. *Competitive Advantage through People: Unleashing the Power of the Workforce.* Boston: Harvard Business School Press.

College and University Context for Library Human Resource Management

William C. Welburn

Try this simple exercise. Take out a blank sheet of paper and draw a line down its center. On the left-hand side of the paper write a short list of topics that define the mission and core values of an academic library. On the right-hand side of the paper list a dozen or so things that distinguish colleges and universities from one another, such as enrollment, degrees offered, athletic conferences, or even party atmosphere. Then try to match the left side with the right side of the paper. What you will likely find is that the mission of an academic library and those core values that seemingly transcend institutions vary—often dramatically—for an array of reasons.

Not only do the services and collections of academic libraries vary by circumstance; organizational characteristics, environments, and cultures can profoundly affect the practice of managing human resources and workplace issues. Although it may seem obvious that policies and procedures cannot be moved across the borders of institutions, the impact of environment, culture, and organizational characteristics on managing people in organizations is significant not only in differentiating the experiences of employees but also in how academic libraries can leverage these factors to enhance organizational performance.

This chapter considers how the differences in characteristics, environments, and cultures of colleges and universities affect managing human resources. It is a given that the world of colleges and universities in the United States is not monolithic. Higher education mirrors the demography and values of the broader society, and the extent to which academic libraries evolve as learning organizations depends on the integration of two important ideas: the degree to which libraries become organizations where "great people can actually *use* their talents" and the extent to which managers and staff understand how their libraries and parent institutions differ from one another in character, culture, and environment (O'Reilly and Pfeffer 2000, 2).

These factors can be formally defined distinctions, such as affiliation, size, or degrees offered. Yet there are other features that are as profound in characterizing colleges and universities, including such environmental and cultural factors as whether a campus is residential or commuter, urban or rural, or whether faculty and staff live close to campus. Students, faculty, librarians, and others who live and work in different colleges and universities are attracted to their locales and identity as much as to more conventional characteristics, and the success of newcomers' professional and social adjustment depends on their capacity to embrace the ethos of the campus.

Different Characteristics, Different Environments, Different Cultures

Different characteristics, environments, and cultures can provide a framework for understanding the opportunities for valuing and involving employees in college and university libraries. These dimensions of diversity may appear obvious if not intuitive. However, they are societal and cultural factors over which academic libraries and their administrators have little control.

Perhaps most familiar among all approaches to differentiating between colleges and universities in the United States is the tallying characteristics. Institutional affiliation (public or private), research or liberal arts, and degrees granted are among the most familiar characteristics employed in describing the differences that exist among colleges and universities. For more than thirty years, the Carnegie Foundation for the Advancement of Teaching has published and revised its classification of American colleges and universities. In the foreword to the 2000 edition of the *Carnegie Classification*, Foundation president Alexander McCormick wrote: "By 2005 we intend to put in place a Classification system that will replace the present single scheme with a series of classifications that will recognize the many dimensions of institutional commonality and difference" (McCormick, 2000). Specifically, the *Carnegie Classification* categorizes 3,941 institutions of higher education, including public and private doctoral/research universities, master's colleges and universities, and baccalaureate colleges representing more than 47.5 percent of America's higher educational institutions; 1,669 associate's colleges; 766 specialized institutions (including but not limited to freestanding seminaries, medical schools, and schools of engineering, business, art, and law); and 28 tribal colleges and universities.

Based on statistical information drawn from the National Center for Education Statistics (NCES) Integrated Postsecondary Education Data System (IPEDS), the *Carnegie Classification* uses a web of criteria that is, as McCormick has noted, "Necessarily retrospective for several reasons. . . . It requires objective data about institutional behavior, which necessitates a look backward in time; data on degree conferrals reflect the completion of educational programs, and thus tell us about educational activities in the past; and Time lags exist between the conferral of degrees and the collection, editing, and release of national data on conferrals by all institutions" (McCormick 2000).

In other words, distinctions made by the Carnegie Foundation are primarily empirical and retrospective, using descriptive data about the number of doctoral degrees conferred across an empirically defined number of disciplines, the number of master's degrees awarded, the proportion of students earning liberal arts degrees, or the percentage of degrees offered in a single field relative to all fields of study available within the institution. Empirically driven distinctions result in a set of discrete categories that have been revised several times; however, the power and authority of the *Carnegie Classification* have profoundly influenced the way policy makers, researchers, and the media have defined American higher education.

Such methods of creating distinctions permeate our thinking about higher education. They form the basis for the decennial surveys of research doctoral programs conducted by the National Research Council, by *U.S. News and World Report* in its rankings of colleges and universities, and the ways in which individual disciplines rank leading academic programs (Morse and Flanigan, 2003). Criteria-based measures are used by the Association of College and Research Libraries in its annual report, *Academic Library Trends and Statistics* (ACRL), and in determining membership eligibility in the Association of Research Libraries (ARL). Yet such measures only form a part of the puzzle in differentiating between colleges and universities. There are other ways to distinguish between higher educational institutions that are pertinent to human resource management in academic libraries. It can be argued that differing environments and cultures in higher education are important—if not crucial—background to encouraging academic libraries to use the talents of their employees, and that library managers may find value in shifting their attention to the environmental and cultural landscapes of their organizations.

The mere location of a college or university represents a rubric for distinguishing higher educational institutions that significantly affects not only student enrollment but also the composition of the workforce. Geographic distinctions, such as urban/suburban/rural or region, have a clear influence on the available workforce and its diversity. As noted in the 2002–2003 *Chronicle of Higher Education Almanac*, there are substantial distinctions state-by-state in the number of colleges and universities, with as many as 419 and 117 in California and Massachusetts and as few as 9 and 15 in Wyoming and Nevada, respectively (2002). Significant state-by-state differences can also be observed in such characteristics of college student enrollment as the proportion of college students enrolled full-time and the percentage of college students from minority groups. Some metropolitan areas, such as Boston, New York, and Philadelphia, have large concentrations of private and public colleges, whereas states such as California maintain an extensive and integrated network of state universities and community colleges.

Yet there are more subtle distinctions that affect personnel. These include demographic characteristics of the available local workforce and of the community; logistics of negotiating a community—including distance from home to work; economic factors such as cost of living; and the political, social, and cultural environments of the campus and its community.

One other dimension of environment has to do with the intraorganizational life of a library and its association with the campus. College and university libraries are differentiated not only by the location and fiscal support for the academic library as a physical and virtual space on campus, but also in the provision of physical space and proximity of employees to one another in the workplace and to library users. This is an issue of special importance for library human resources administrators as they consider technological requirements in the workplace.[1]

Closely associated with environment are those differences in institutional culture that affect academic libraries and the shaping of their organizational cultures. Culture, Edgar Schein wrote, "manifests itself at three levels: the level of deep tacit assumptions that are the essence of the culture, the level of espoused values that often reflect what a group wishes ideally to be and the way it wants to present itself publicly, and the day-to-day behavior that represents a complex compromise among the espoused values, the deeper assumptions, and the immediate requirements of the situation" (1996, 11). Organizational cultures, in Schein's view, are based on shared histories, experiences, and assumptions of employees. But, as Schein continues, there are "occupational cultures" that transcend organizations: "The various functional cultures in organizations are, in fact, partly the result of membership in broader cross-organizational occupational communities. Salespeople the world over, accountants, assembly line workers, and engineers share some tacit assumptions about the nature of their work regardless of who their particular employer is at any given time" (1996, 11).

Throughout higher education there is an intersection between organizational or institutional and professional cultures. This intersection illustrates a paradox between cohesion of organization and maintenance of professional identity.[2] To some extent, we define human resource management in academic libraries by the standards of our profession, as evidenced by guidelines published by professional associations and by the agenda of conferences and workshops. Yet we are also bound by the differences in the cultures of our institutions that directly affect our capacity to enact human resources activities.

In *Bright College Years*, Anne Matthews writes that colleges and universities enjoy "powerful double lives, one daily and real, another conducted largely in the national imagination" (1997, 17). Cultural differences among American colleges and universities largely fall along the fault lines between myth and reality, between the values espoused and experiences of adaptation to circumstances. Ivy League universities and New England liberal arts colleges enjoy real and imagined cultures of selectivity and liberal education. Midwestern public universities are imagined to have vast academic offerings and competitive athletic programs. Colleges and universities residing along the coasts of Florida and California conjure images of cultures of work and play. The mid-Atlantic region's Division I Patriot League has attempted to invoke an image of the scholar-athlete among member institutions, and many of its members continue to refrain from offering athletic scholarships. League director Carolyn Schlie Femovich said of the Patriot League: "We're still creating our history, and a sense of where we want to be. I think it's clear what we stand for" (in Suggs 2002, A40). Real or imagined, these images affect the choices of prospective students and employees as they consider the fit between themselves and the academic communities they choose to become a part of.

Implications for Academic Libraries

The implications of the impact of distinctive characteristics, environments, and cultures are substantial on the formation, development, and refinement of human resources in academic libraries. Differences among institutions of higher education affect a range of workplace and human resources issues and strategies, including recruitment and retention, policy formation, and the possibility of transferring ideas and models across institutional boundaries.

Geographic location remains a prominent factor in recruiting new librarians, and an array of specific reasons for success or failure can be given, including cost of living relative to salary, mobility of prospective employees, proximity of cities, and distance from home to work. Yet there are other environmental and cultural considerations for a prospective employee. A newcomer might ask, "Will I fit into the organizational culture?" In other words, what must the newcomer sacrifice to grow professionally as a part of the library staff?

There is an intersection between environment and culture in designing physical workspaces for librarians and other staff. As Marilyn Thomas noted, "For libraries engaged in team structures, each staff member's work area must allow for any of the task they might do. Occasionally, this might mean a square footage equal to a higher-ranking staff member who is not totally reliant on electronic information for their managerial work." (2000, 414). A library with a commitment to a team-based culture will likely consider the physical environment in fostering teamwork among employees. The environment enacted may likely affect the job satisfaction of individual employees relative to their buy-in to the team-based environment. Some will stay, while others are likely to leave.

There is also an important meeting point between library and institutional personnel and human resource policies, many of which are linked to environmental and cultural considerations, and the capacity of a library to transfer models and ideas across institutional boundaries. Human resource policies and practices may be grounded in such characteristics as institutional affiliation (public or private, religious); environmental adaptations such as available office space, parking, or on-campus housing for staff; or cultural considerations that range from definitions of academic status to intra-institutional policies on the value of and support for professional development.

Conclusion

At the end of *Bright College Years*, Anne Matthews describes dress and the ritual of college and university commencements:

> Increasingly, graduation dress varies at U.S. campuses. At Northern Arizona University, many Indian seniors accept their diplomas in buckskin dresses or fringed boots. At the University of Hawaii, leis blaze above the academic black. African-American graduates may decide to wear kente-cloth stoles, splendidly striped in red and black and gold and green. . . . At Henry Cogswell College in Washington State, the graduating class, all fourteen of them, fit nicely into a freight elevator; at the University of Texas—Austin, graduates must rise stadium section by stadium section. (1997, 268–69)

The ritual of graduation is one of many ways to draw distinctions in American higher education. It is powerfully symbolic and rich in metaphors reflecting institutional culture. It is also yet another manifestation—albeit superficial—of the importance of differences among institutions of higher learning throughout the United States. Such differences, whether cultural, environmental, or institutional, shape the way work is accomplished by librarians, faculty, and staff in their communal effort to support learning and advances in scholarship. Recognizing the function of institutional characteristics, environment, and culture in attracting and managing employees is vital to establishing and sustaining human resources programs in academic libraries.

Notes

1. See Barney (1996) and Hatch (1987).

2. For further discussion of conflict between the individual and community in higher education, see Weick (1983).

References

Barney, Alan. 1996. "The Impact of Technology on Library Space Requirements." *LIBRES: Library and Information Science Research* 6 (June). Available: http://libres.curtin.edu.au/libre6n1/barney.htm. (Accessed April 29, 2003).

Chronicle of Higher Education 2002–03 Almanac. 2002. Available: http://chronicle.com/free/almanac/2002/index.htm. (Accessed April 29, 2003).

Hatch, Mary Jo. 1987. "Physical Barriers, Task Characteristics and Interaction Activities in Research and Development Firms." *Administrative Science Quarterly* 32: 387–99.

Matthews, Anne. 1997. *Bright College Years: Inside the American Campus Today.* New York: Simon & Schuster.

McCormick, Alexander. [2000]. *The 2000 Carnegie Classification: Background and Description.* Available: http://www.carnegiefoundation. org/Classification/CIHE2000/background.htm. (Accessed April 29, 2003).

Morse, Robert J., and Samuel M. Flanigan. 2003. "How We Rank Schools." *America's Best Colleges.* Available: http://www.usnews. com/usnews/edu/college/rankings/about/03rank.htm. (Accessed April 29, 2003).

O'Reilly, Charles A., III, and Jeffrey Pfeffer. 2000. *Hidden Value: How Great Companies Achieve Extraordinary Results with Ordinary People.* Boston: Harvard Business School Press.

Schein, Edgar. 1996. "Three Cultures of Management: The Key to Organizational Learning." *Sloan Management Review* 38 (Fall): 9–20.

Suggs, Welch. 2002. "The Patriot League's Grand Experiment." *Chronicle of Higher Education* (March 29): A40.

Thomas, Mary Augusta. 2000. "Redefining Library Space: Managing the Co-existence of Books, Computers, and Readers." *Journal of Academic Librarianship* 26/6 (November): 408–15.

Weick, Karl E. 1983. "Contradictions in a Community of Scholars: the Cohesion-Accuracy Tradeoff." *Review of Higher Education* 6 (Summer): 253–67.

2

Creating and Sustaining a Diverse Workplace

Janice Simmons-Welburn

Diversity as a word and a value continues to figure prominently in the public rhetoric of academic institutions across the United States. Colleges and universities, regardless of size, institutional affiliation, and population served, continue to spend a considerable amount of time in conversation about diversity, wrestling with their thoughts over the effects of diversity on classrooms and residence halls, in libraries and student life, and the work of administrators, faculty, and staff.

Yet, to paraphrase the question David A. Thomas and Robin J. Ely (1996, 80) raised in an article published in the *Harvard Business Review*, why should academic libraries concern themselves with diversity? What follows is predicated on an assumption that academic libraries, like their parent organizations and organizations stretching across society, desire to move beyond the surface clichés of diversity that spotlight differences by ethnicity, gender, nationality, or sexual identity, to consider a kind of diversity that brings individual experience, backgrounds, and cultures together to work collaboratively to define and achieve common missions for libraries in higher education.

Diversity in its most basic form represents the existence and recognition of the presence of differences within a given environment or situation. The word itself implies a dynamic to be understood in relation to communication or interaction between individuals or groups within a shared space. Or, as Clifford Geertz put it in the context of cultural anthropology, "the puzzles raised by the fact of cultural diversity have more to do with our capacity to feel our way into alien sensibilities, modes of thought we do not possess, and are not likely to, than they do with whether we can escape preferring our own preferences" (1985, 110). University of Illinois Chancellor Nancy Cantor explained in a keynote address before the Third National Conference on Diversity in Academic Libraries that the source of inspiration to create diverse communities out of colleges and universities resides in three important assumptions:

- The University is a public good

- Libraries are prototypical public goods . . . they exemplify the values of exploration, preservation, and community

- Diversity is central to the core missions of universities and academic libraries . . . universities and academic libraries cannot serve the public good unless they learn the fundamental lesson of diversity (2002)

Cantor asserted that the challenge for colleges and universities and their libraries entailed an intertwining of diversity and academic excellence, and the responsibility of librarians, faculty, administrators, and others who work in higher education is to maintain the interaction between the two. The social context for academic libraries is profoundly affected by significant changes occurring on campuses, including ever increasing diversity of students and faculty, and continual rethinking of the cultures of many disciplines that have affected scholarship and teaching. In turn, as Cantor has suggested, academic libraries are poised to affect scholarship and learning. These changes signal the need to retain diversity as a core value in libraries and, specifically, how in a human resources context libraries are developed as learning organizations.

Diversity provides libraries with an opportunity for organizational development through collaboration and team-based decision making and implementation of ideas to meet the challenges of teaching, learning, and scholarship throughout higher educational institutions. Rather than portray workplace diversity within the context of compliance, it can become an organizing principle closely associated with the process of continuous learning.

This chapter follows a different trajectory from the central themes usually found in published writings on valuing and managing diversity in academic libraries. Specifically, the strengths and weaknesses of past and present perspectives influencing our agenda on diversity as a workplace issue are explored, followed by further consideration of the implications of all three perspectives for human resources.

What Is Diversity?

Diversity as a workplace construct has been defined in various ways. In the view of Robin Ely and David Thomas, diversity "is a characteristic of groups of two or more people and typically refers to demographic differences of one sort or another among group members" (2001, 230). Taylor Cox defines diversity as a workplace issue as "the variation of social and cultural identities among people existing together in a defined employment or market setting" (2001, 3). More specifically, cultural diversity "means the representation, in one social system, of people with distinctly different group affiliations of cultural significance" (Cox 1994, 6). Using these definitions, identity is related to situation, organization, or circumstance. In this context diversity becomes dynamic in an organization when one begins to think in terms of managing diversity; workplace behaviors are affected by policies and practices within the organization.

Three different perceptions of the meaning of diversity in the workplace are explored in this chapter. They include (1) the relationship between diversity and affirmative action and (2) arguments presented by a paradigm of changing populations. Finally, a third perspective, advanced by Ely and Thomas, who view diversity as "the varied perspectives and approaches to work that members of different identity groups bring" (2001, 80), is explored in contrast to the aforementioned perceptions of what diversity is and how strategies can be built to support it.

Is Affirmative Action Diversity?

Cox defined affirmative action in practice as "the explicit use of a person's group identity as a criterion in making selection decisions" (1994, 250). As Cox maintains, affirmative action is not the use of quotas or the selection and advancement of employees who are fundamentally unqualified. Nor is affirmative action reverse discrimination. Affirmative action rests on what Lyndon Johnson meant by "freedom is not enough" when he outlined the underpinnings of affirmative action in his historic commencement address at Howard University:

> To this end equal opportunity is essential, but not enough, not enough. Men and women of all races are born with the same range of abilities. But ability is not just the product of birth. Ability is stretched or stunted by the family that you live with, and the neighborhood you live in—by the school you go to and the poverty or the richness of your surroundings. It is the product of a hundred unseen forces playing upon the little infant, the child, and finally the man. (1965)

Affirmative action is not, then, synonymous with diversity. Affirmative action is, as Johnson maintained, a mechanism for righting historical wrongs. It is an effort to turn the actions of the civil rights movement into policy designed to end discrimination and assert fairness beyond merely securing equal opportunity. Its purpose, as Stephen Steinberg suggests, is "to break down the wall of occupational segregation that excluded racial minorities and women from entire occupational sectors throughout American history" (2002, 37).

Affirmative action also has its limitations. It is at best a short-term strategy or sequence of strategies to accomplish a broader vision, whether to achieve diversity, equal opportunity, or social justice. In an organizational context, affirmative action can provide the requisite framework to ensure fairness in hiring and promotion practices by establishing a reach into populations underrepresented among employees. However, affirmative action is substantially limited in providing long-term, structural change once the walls have been broken down.

Affirmative action is also subject to litigation. Since the early 1970s, the landscape of affirmative action—from hiring practices to contract awards to college admissions—has been riddled with court decisions and referenda that have tightened the parameters of recruitment and admissions practices. For example, although *Bakke v. the University of California Board of Regents* (1978) questioned the validity of the shadow of slavery and segregation on racial preference in college admissions decisions, the Supreme Court's verdict retained justification for considering race as a factor. Court decisions such as *Taxman v. The Board of Education for Piscataway Township* and *Adarand Constructors, Inc. v. PeZa* have also blurred the rights of employers to use race respectively in hiring practices and in awarding contracts to minority-owned companies.

Finally, given its legal history, affirmative action is clearly the source of substantial conflict in organizations. Despite the aim of organizations to reduce if not resolve its potential, conflict indeed arises when an employee is seen as someone who was hired and advanced for affirmative action purposes.

Workforce 2000

Diversity has also been cast in the context of the changing demographics of the United States and the desire to make every organization mirror the broader society. Specifically, changing demographics are likely to influence the character of the U.S. labor market and growth in the labor force in relation to knowledge and skill requirements for twenty-first-century jobs. Studies have found that human resource administrators are "paying more attention to the active recruitment of new workers to fill job openings. A recent survey of human resource executives found that 54% reported skilled labor shortages which they expected to continue into the future," and that recruitment was among the highest of priorities for corporate offices of human resources (Lommel 1999, 1). In 1987, the Hudson Institute's heavily cited report, *Workforce 2000,* was completed for the U.S. Department of Labor. It predicted that there would be a growing gap between the skills and needs in the changing economy and changing demographics of the American workforce.

What captured the attention of many organizations were the significant changes anticipated in the demographic character of the United States. The nation's population, so the argument goes, is becoming increasingly diverse. Accordingly, various institutions such as school systems and colleges and universities must better prepare tomorrow's workforce. Yet even *Workforce 2020* (Judy and D'Amico 1997)—the successor to the original report—suggests that those anticipated changes will arrive more slowly and evolutionarily than was originally predicted. The consequences—technological challenges in the workplace, an aging population, global competition in the economy, and ethnic diversity—will likely require a strong commitment to improving education, especially at primary and secondary levels.

There are several important weaknesses to this approach to diversity. First, it is built on projections of demographic changes and shortages in various labor sectors. Peter Drucker has noted that demographic forecasts are themselves subject to change (2002, 250–51). The argument depends all too heavily on the realization of such shortages in a world of uncertainty that includes the ebb and flow of immigrant populations to the United States; the next technological innovation around the corner; and economic factors affecting federal, state, and local governments.

There is an additional weakness to the changing demographics argument. This perspective assumes readiness among populations to assume a role in a knowledge-based society. One Workforce 2020 Conference participant purportedly said: "We cannot continue to talk about our competitiveness in the world without talking about our work force. We can't talk about our work force without talking about education. In turn, we can't talk about education without recognizing the serious shortcomings in the existing system" (Lommel 1999). In a completely different context, *New York Times* columnist Bob Herbert wrote: "Education is the food that nourishes the nation's soul. When public officials refuse to provide adequate school resources for the young, it's the same as parents refusing to feed their children" (2003, A31).Given present inequities in financial support for education both between and within school systems and in educational attainment grounded in barriers to opportunity, the infusion of diverse populations in a knowledge-based economy will lag behind the opportunities that the economy may present.

Different Voices, Shared Minds

Cox has suggested that to be effective in organizational development and performance diversity must be a value added activity. Not only must diversity improve organizational values,

> well-managed diversity can add value to an organization by (1) improving problem solving, (2) increasing creativity and innovation, (3) increasing organizational flexibility, (4) improving the quality of personnel through better recruitment and retention, and (5) improving marketing strategies, especially for organizations that sell products or services to end users. (2001, 6)

Ely and Thomas provide a third perspective on how diversity can best be achieved in organizations in what they call an "integration and learning perspective." A very process-oriented model, the integration and learning perspective exploits the

> insights, skills, and experiences employees have developed as members of various cultural identity groups (that) are potentially valuable resources that the work group can use to rethink its primary tasks and redefine its markets, products, strategies, and business practices in ways that will advance its mission. This perspective links diversity to work processes . . . in a manner that makes diversity a resource for learning and adaptive change. (2001, 240)

In other words, the benefits derived from achieving a diverse organization are involvement and, ultimately, the power of newcomers to affect organizational change by inserting employees into the center of decisions and organizational action. By extension, this model opens opportunities for employees from different backgrounds to advance into greater positions of authority within the organization. Thus it assumes willingness on the part of employees to relinquish the reins and share decision-making authority. As James Williams has noted, the Ely and Thomas model relies on the preconditions of receptivity among leadership and in organizational culture (1999, 37).

This model also assumes that organizations will continue to develop and utilize strategies for recruiting new employees, many of which will continue to rely on affirmative action policies and procedures to remove barriers in hiring and promotion practices. If, for example, race is outlawed as a factor in deciding whom to hire or advance, then achieving the kind of integration in learning suggested by this model becomes increasingly difficult to achieve.

Next Steps for Library Human Resource Administrators

We return to the question raised at the beginning of our essay: Why should academic libraries concern themselves with diversity? If the work of Robin Ely, David A. Thomas, Taylor Cox, R. Roosevelt Thomas, and other organizational researchers can be used for guidance, then there is substantial evidence that effective strategies for making diversity work in academic libraries and other organizations contribute to the vitality of the organization and to organizational effectiveness. If Nancy Cantor is correct when she asserts that there is an intertwining of diversity and academic excellence, diversity becomes central to the mission of academic libraries and their parent institutions, and it also functions as an organizing principle for academic library leaders and human resource administrators. There are several important aspects of the discussion surrounding diversity that can be considered.

First, affirmative action may indeed have a short future. Court cases decided after referenda were passed have narrowed the parameters so that affirmative action policies and programs are more difficult to manage. However, in his defense of affirmative action, sociologist Orlando Patterson wrote that affirmative action provides an opportunity for access to "the network-rich educational institutions of the nation and the self-generating career networks at the workplace" (1998, 22).[1]

Despite the controversies surrounding it, affirmative action's policy and practices provide academic libraries with a framework for facilitating recruitment and organizational entry into the profession, specifically to academic libraries. In the spirit of President Clinton's "mend it don't end it," affirmative action policies and programs will likely shift from exclusive to inclusive strategies as a natural evolution of the breaking down of barriers to employment in libraries and as a consequence of recent litigation. Programs such as minority residency and scholarships were effective in the 1990s; however, strategies designed to build more inclusion are likely to evolve over the next few years, due in part to the litigious environment but also in an effort to put an "integration and learning perspective" into practice.

Second, while affirmative action strategies in libraries—such as residency programs and overt attempts to recruit minority students—can be viewed as short-term efforts, longer-term structural and process changes that make diversity work are dependent on the leadership inertia of academic library administrators and staff alike, both within library organizations and in professional associations. James Williams reminds us, "Excellent diversity programs evolve from excellent diversity plans, and it is through these programs that many comprehensive, strategic and long-range change efforts are now in place throughout academe to assist monocultural organizations in the transition to multicultural organizations"(1999, 47). Such planning initiatives can ultimately affect the longer-term, strategic direction of an organization when they are linked to decision processes involving diverse groups.

There are tremendous openings to make diversity work through the development of team-based organizations that use process as an opportunity to grow ideas that advance an organization. This approach to diversity is closely related to civility. "Civility," Stephen Carter argues, "is the sum of the many sacrifices we are called to make for the sake of living together. [Civility] adds value to the better society we are struggling together through our differences to build" (1998, 25). In the workplace, civility is fundamental to our efforts to collaborate or work in teams. Failure to address incivility compromises our efforts to maintain organization, affects morale and productivity, and ultimately harms our attempts at working together to build community between our libraries and the rest of our colleges or universities. "Different voices, shared minds" also means that we will respect different voices and respond to one another with courtesy and respect. Incivility, like racism, sexism, or homophobia, often can be subtle rather than blatant. As learning organizations, libraries will need to incorporate civility as a basic premise for achieving diversity and implementing effective strategies to achieve organizational goals.

Notes

1.   Although Patterson's argument focuses on African Americans, his specific concern for access to networks may have broader, albeit limited, application.

References

Cantor, Nancy. 2002. Keynote address: *Diversity: Building a Strategic Future.* The Third National Conference on Diversity in Academic Libraries, April 4–6. Available: http://www.lib.uiowa.edu/cicdiversity/papers.html. (Accessed June 3, 2003).

Carter, Stephen L. 1998. *Civility.* New York: Basic Books.

Cox, Taylor. 1994. *Cultural Diversity in Organizations: Theory, Research & Practice.* San Francisco: Berrett-Koehler.

Cox, Taylor. 2001. *Creating the Multicultural Organization: A Strategy for Capturing the Power of Diversity.* San Francisco: Jossey-Bass.

Drucker, Peter. 2002. *Managing in the Next Society.* New York: St. Martin's Press.

Ely, Robin J., and David A. Thomas. 2001. "Cultural Diversity at Work: the Effects of Diversity Perspectives on Work Group Processes and Outcomes." *Administrative Science Quarterly* 46: 229–73.

Geertz, Clifford. 1985. "The Uses of Diversity and the Future of Ethnocentrism." *Michigan Quarterly Review* 25 (Winter): 105–23.

Herbert, Bob. 2003. "The War on Schools." *New York Times* (March 6): A31.

Johnson, Lyndon B. 1965."To Fulfill These Rights." Commencement Address at Howard University, delivered June 4. Available: http://www.lbjlib.utexas.edu/johnson/archives.hom/speeches.hom/650604.asp. (Accessed June 3, 2003).

Johnstone, William B., and Arnold Packer. 1987. *Workforce 2000: Work and Workers for the Twenty-First Century.* Indianapolis, IN: Hudson Institute.

Judy, Richard W., and Carol D'Amico. 1997. *Workforce 2020: Work and Workers in the 21st Century.* Indianapolis, IN: Hudson Institute.

Lommel, Jane M. 1999. "Workforce 2020 Conference Summary." *Chicago Fed Letter* No. 140a (April): 1–4.

Patterson, Orlando. 1998. "Affirmative Action: Opening Up Workplace Networks to Afro-Americans." *Brookings Review* 16 (Spring): 22–23.

Steinberg, Stephen. 2001. "Mending Affirmative Action." In *Who's Qualified?* Edited by Lani Guinier and Susan Sturm. Boston: Beacon Press.

Thomas, David A., and Robin J. Ely. 1996. "Making Differences Matter: A New Paradigm for Managing Diversity." *Harvard Business Review* 74 (September/October): 79–91.

Williams, James F., II. 1999. "Managing Diversity: Library Management in Light of the Dismantling of Affirmative Action." *Journal of Library Administration* 27: 27–48.

New Hires in Research Libraries: Demographic Trends and Hiring Priorities*

Stanley J. Wilder

Thousands of librarians will be retiring in the next ten years,[1] and when they do, they will take with them a vast supply of accumulated expertise, leaving behind a host of new staffing and organizational issues. The approaching wave of retirements may be the most important human resources phenomenon facing the profession, but it is a phenomenon over which the library community will have virtually no control. We can no more manage the retirements in our ranks than we can the weather.

The real management issue resulting from retirements is replacements: How can librarianship recruit new entrants to the profession in sufficient numbers, quality, and expertise to replace its retirees? This chapter addresses one small portion of this question, by describing demographic trends among those recently hired at ARL member libraries and the kinds of positions they fill. The data used to support this analysis come from the electronic data sets from ARL's Salary Survey, from 1980 to 2000.

New Hires

New hires are the single most important indicator of the health and future direction of libraries. (In this study, a "new hire" is an individual in the Salary Survey data with a value of 0 or 1 in the variable "years in library.") They signal the ability of libraries to either afford or recruit new staff, but more important, they provide a snapshot of the kinds of expertise sought at a given point in time.

Number

There were 1,079 new hires in 2000, up 35 percent from just two years before. (See Table 3.1.) The 2000 figure marks the highest level in the available data. New hires in Canadian ARL libraries, however, have increased only slightly, and continue to lag well behind those in the United States.

Table 3.1. Number of New Hires and Percentage of Population by Year: Canada, United States, and Total

	Canada		United States		Total	
Year	Number	Percent	Number	Percent	Number	Percent
1986	28	3.4	834	12.1	862	13.0
1990	49	5.8	1,009	13.4	1,058	15.1
1994	24	2.9	778	10.5	802	10.8
1998	22	3.1	775	10.1	797	11.0
2000	31	4.1	1,048	12.9	1,079	14.4

Hiring Priorities for New Hires

Hiring priorities changed substantially between 1985 and 2000. Table 3.2 presents the top six job categories among new hires in 1985 and compares their numbers to 2000. Note that the overall ARL population grew by 18 percent in this period.

Table 3.2. Top Six New-Hire Job Categories, 1985 Compared to 2000

	1985		2000		
	Number of New Hires	Percent of New Hires	Number of New Hires	Percent of New Hires	Percent Change
Reference Librarian	214	25.27	322	29.84	50
Cataloger	154	18.18	84	7.78	−45
Functional Specialist	82	9.68	243	22.52	196
Public Services	75	8.85	47	4.36	−37
Subject Specialist	59	6.97	95	8.80	61
Head, Other	58	6.85	76	7.04	31

The most dramatic change in Table 3.2 is the burgeoning number of functional specialists, now the second largest job category among new hires. If one compares the rate of growth of functional specialist new hires between 1990 and 2000 to that of reference librarians and then projects that growth into the future, we find that new hires for functional specialist positions overtook those for reference by 2003.

What is a functional specialist? According to the instructions for the 2000 survey, functional specialists are

> media specialists, or . . . experts in management fields such as personnel, fiscal matters, systems, preservation, etc. Specialists may not be, strictly speaking, professional librarians (i.e., have the MLS). The "specialist" category would generally not be used for someone with significant supervisory responsibilities, who should instead be listed as a department head or assistant director. (Kyrillidou and O'Connor 2000, 99)[1]

In 1998, 61 percent of new hires in functional specialist positions were hired for systems analysis/programming positions, and the remainder were spread among eight other job specializations. Functional specialists are thus predominantly individuals hired for IT-related positions.

Library Degree

It has become common that new hires to ARL professional positions have no library degree. In 1985, just 7 percent of new hires had no such degree, but this figure grew steadily, to 20 percent in 2000. This trend is fueled in part by the growth in hires to functional specialist positions. In 2000, 48 percent of functional specialists had no library degree, compared to just 12 percent of other job categories.

Minorities

The minority portion of the overall population has changed little since 1985, but there has been steady progress in the percentage of minorities among new hires. (See Table 3.3, page 22.) For example, the Hispanic percentage of the new-hire population more than doubled between 1985 and 2000, while the Asian American and African American percentages nearly doubled. The increase in the number of minorities among new hires is a measure of success for the diversity efforts of ARL libraries, but it may be some time before these numbers have an appreciable affect on the overall ARL population.

Table 3.3. Number and Percentage of New Hires by Race/Ethnicity

	Number of New Hires					
	1985	1986	1990	1994	1998	2000
Caucasian/Other	738	757	886	778	671	886
Minority	68	77	122	96	104	162
African American	31	34	41	36	37	67
Hispanic	7	11	29	17	16	26
Asian or Pacific Islander	29	29	50	43	48	67
American Indian or Native Alaskan	1	3	2	0	3	2

	Percentage of New Hires					
	1985	1986	1990	1994	1998	2000
Caucasian/Other	91.6	90.8	87.9	87.7	86.6	84.5
Minority	8.4	9.2	12.1	12.3	13.4	15.5
African American	3.8	4.1	4.1	4.6	4.8	6.4
Hispanic	0.9	1.3	2.9	2.2	2.1	2.5
Asian or Pacific Islander	3.6	3.5	5.0	5.5	6.2	6.4
American Indian or Native Alaskan	0.1	0.4	0.2		0.4	0.2

New Professionals

"New professionals" are a subset of new hires; they are new hires who have a value of 0 or 1 in ARL's "years experience" variable. The number of new professionals increased consistently at about 12 percent per year between 1996 and 2000. (See Table 3.4.) Between 1980 and 2000, the number of new professionals peaked at 495, in 1989. Although the 2000 figure of 447 is the second highest number since 1980, there has been little change in the level of new professionals as a percentage of the overall population.

Table 3.4. Number of New Professionals and
Percentage of Population by Year

Year	New Professionals	Percentage of Population
1980	369	5.6
1981	306	4.6
1982	316	3.9
1983	277	4.4
1984	314	5.5
1985	415	4.5
1986	347	4.8
1987	383	4.9
1988	393	6.0
1989	495	5.1
1990	425	4.0
1991	330	3.7
1992	304	3.8
1993	312	4.1
1994	334	3.8
1995	308	3.4
1996	286	3.6
1997	302	4.0
1998	338	4.6
1999	392	5.1
2000	447	5.6

Movement Between Libraries

The ARL data cannot produce actual turnover rates, but they do provide one interesting, albeit limited, approximation. By using the variables "years of professional experience" and "years in library," one can determine the number of individuals at each experience level who have worked at only one library in the course of their professional careers. Table 3.5 presents the results of this analysis for staff with zero to five years of professional experience.

Table 3.5. Number and Percentage of Staff Who Have Worked in Only One Library, 2000

Years of Experience	Number	Percentage
0	77	100
1	304	87
2	254	59
3	272	58
4	215	42
5	243	37

There are two potential explanations for the sharp drop-off in Table 3.5. First, individuals hired into ARL libraries as new professionals may tend to change libraries soon thereafter. Second, ARL libraries do substantial hiring of individuals in the first five years of their professional careers. For example, in 2000, 25 percent of new hires had between two and five years of professional experience. The simplest explanation for this phenomenon may lie in life cycle factors not entirely under the control of library managers.

Hiring Priorities for New Professionals

Table 3.6 illustrates that functional specialists have supplanted catalogers among new professionals, as well as among new hires.

Two Futures

Cataloging and functional specialist positions provide two divergent perspectives on the meaning of the trends shown above, one troubling, one encouraging.

Cataloging

In 1986, professional staff in cataloging were among the youngest groups reported in the ARL data. This is not surprising, given cataloging's traditional role as one of two major entry points for new professionals. For example, reference and cataloging alone accounted for 64 percent of all new professionals hired in 1985. Just fourteen years later, the cataloging population became one of the oldest groups. In 2000, 32 percent of catalogers were aged fifty-five and over, a proportion almost twice as large as that of the comparable reference population.

**Table 3.6. Top Six New-Professional Job Categories,
1983 Compared to 2000**

	1983		2000		
	Number	Percent	Number	Percent	Percent Change
Reference Librarian	77	27.8	156	34.9	103
Cataloger	70	25.3	38	8.5	−46
Public Services	38	13.7	25	5.6	−34
Subject Specialist	25	9.0	34	7.6	36
Functional Specialist	22	7.9	137	30.6	523
Technical Services	22	7.9	15	3.4	−32

The aging of the cataloging population, unusual even by ARL standards, is almost certainly the result of a remarkable drop-off in hiring. Between 1985 and 2000, the number of new hires to cataloging positions dropped 45 percent, and of new professionals by 64 percent. The drop in hiring for cataloging positions, together with the high retirement rate, almost certainly accounts for the drop in the overall number of catalogers, down 28 percent in this same period. Clearly, libraries are diverting resources away from staffing professional cataloging positions, and the data provide no hint as to when and at what level the downward spiral will end.

The advanced age of catalogers is cause for concern that libraries may not be able to replace their exiting catalogers, even given a reduced level of need. It is also possible that reduced hiring for cataloging in recent years has had an effect on library education, leading to a de-emphasis on cataloging in the curriculum and reduced numbers of students taking up the discipline (Spillane 1999).

Functional Specialists

However, impending retirements provide some opportunities as well as threats. The burgeoning of the IT-dominated functional specialist job category brings to mind the last great generational shift, the staffing boom that brought thousands of people into librarianship in the 1960s and 1970s. That generation also brought new skills to a changing profession in a way that appears now to have been healthy, even necessary.

Through concerted efforts over the past thirty years, libraries have succeeded in reducing their need for some forms of library expertise. Yet at the same time they have developed needs for new kinds of expertise. Librarianship is fortunate that, as information undergoes its first revolution since Gutenberg, the profession appears positioned to take on substantial numbers of new people with new skills to help it adapt. In this view, there is no cause for alarm if functional specialists do not look more like traditional librarians. In fact, the long-term interest of librarianship may make those differences necessary, just as they were for the generation before them. Now, as before, the kids are all right.

Or the kids will be all right, provided there are enough of them. The profession's most important task is to bring fresh ideas to bear on the questions of professional education, recruitment, and compensation, so as to make librarianship a more attractive choice for young people. For those kids smart enough to make this choice, it only remains for veteran librarians to prepare them for success. It is like parenting, in the sense that these elders can be a living link between librarianship's past and future, transmitting what they know, what they value, and the honorable role they serve in our culture.

Notes

* This chapter was previously published as "New Hires in Research Libraries: Demographic Trends and Hiring Priorities." *ARL* 221 (April 2002): 5–8. Available at: http://www.arl.org/newsltr/221/newhires. html.

1. Approximately 52,000 librarians were aged fifty-five and over in 2000, according to the U.S. Department of Commerce, Bureau of the Census, *Current Population Survey* (Washington, DC: Bureau of the Census, n.d.): table 12, "Employed persons by detailed occupation, sex, and age. Annual Average 2000."

References

Kyrillidou, Martha, and Michael O'Connor, comps. and eds. 2000. *ARL Annual Salary Survey 1999–2000*. Washington, DC: Association of Research Libraries.

Spillane, Jodi Lynn. 1999. "Comparison of Required Introductory Cataloging Courses, 1986 to 1998." *Library Resources & Technical Services* 43, no 4: 223–30.

U.S. Department of Commerce, Bureau of the Census. n.d. *Current Population Survey*. Washington, DC: Bureau of the Census.

4

Recruitment and Selection in Academic Libraries

Laine Stambaugh

How many librarians can spin an anecdotal tale about how they ended up in librarianship? I was a passenger in my brother's car on the way to my grandmother's house one Christmas Day many years ago. I was just completing a master's degree in linguistics and had been working full-time for six years as a senior library clerk at a local community college in California. Prior to that, I'd worked as a student assistant in a university library for three years. As I was talking to my brother about my plans that day (you're going on for yet *another* degree?), he asked me why I didn't consider librarianship as a career "since I'd spent so many years working in a library."

This chapter comments on the current recruitment situation for academic libraries, suggests strategies for recruitment, considers changes to the selection and screening process, and offers advice for a successful interview process.

The Current Library Recruitment Crisis

Recent studies by Stanley Wilder and others indicate an unprecedented number of retirements predicted for the Baby Boomer[1] generation of librarians within the next ten years.[2] At the same time, the number of accredited graduate library and information science programs has been decreasing. Thirty ALA-accredited programs have been suspended or discontinued since 1925—four since 1992—and those programs are producing only slightly more graduates now. Current economic constraints faced by academic libraries also affect the recruitment and retention of a diverse professional staff. According to the *ARL Annual Salary Survey 2001–2002* only 12 percent of U.S. academic professional staff (mainly librarians) are members of ethnic minorities (2002, 8). Although Wilder's data indicate a healthy increase in new ARL minority hires (up from 8.4 to 15.5 percent between 1985 and 2000), it is not enough to keep up with the demographic trend for the projected future population on our academic campuses. The consequences of the inability to recruit those individuals to the profession means less influence on shaping and representing the collections that a research library is intent on building and maintaining, collections that should, in an ideal world, closely reflect the members of our community and society. If young people do not see themselves reflected in the faces of the information professionals with whom they come into contact, they will not be attracted to this profession (Kaufman 2002).

Systematic Recruitment Efforts in Academic Libraries

Becoming an academic librarian has been an "accidental career" for many, including the author of this chapter. It is encouraging, however, that leading professional organizations are taking a systematic look at recruiting the next generation of academic librarians. In 2002–2003, the Association of College and Research Libraries (ACRL) and the Association of Research Libraries (ARL) formed a joint task force charged to *"develop fresh strategies for recruiting and advancing a new generation of talent for the profession of academic librarianship to succeed in the 21st century"* (ACRL 2002–2003). The academic and research library component of @your library ™, the Campaign for America's Libraries, was launched during the 2003 ACRL National Conference. This campaign includes a "toolkit" of materials adaptable to academic institutions, such as the template for creation of a brochure that suggests combining an academic major and librarianship for an exciting academic librarian career. Librarians who perform instruction as well as those who work at public desks could easily pass out those brochures to students and faculty members with whom they come in contact. The brochure would have the name of a librarian or HR officer to contact with questions, thus encouraging a dialogue about the profession that might not have occurred otherwise. Those same brochures could also be passed along to the campus career counselors.

In a recent issue of *CLIR Issues* (Council on Library and Information Resources), the announcement was made that fourteen institutions have offered to "form a network of libraries that will offer yearlong fellowships to provide training in a specialized area of librarianship" (Marcum 2003, 3). The program will offer fellowships to humanists who have recently earned doctoral degrees and will begin in 2004. Trainees will be introduced to the history of academic librarianship and information on current trends in the field. At a time when it appears academic libraries may be eliminating the scholar-librarian positions to make way for other types of information technology specialists (Simmons-Welburn 2000), this is a creative approach to maintaining area specializations and expertise, as well as providing resourceful ways to "grow our own" academic librarians from within academe itself. This will be an important effort to follow as it tracks areas such as special collections, digital library development, and/or area studies development. These future scholars may add a whole new body of knowledge and approaches to the area of scholarly communication. The MLS question will always be debatable in the profession, but in some libraries, scholars such as these have already attained the same credibility on their campuses as within their libraries. In a time of short supply, this may be a practical approach to filling some positions.

In the meantime, academic libraries must no longer rely on "accidental careers" to happen. Academic librarians must take a more active and systematic role in attracting individuals to our profession. There is no doubt that recruitment could be made much easier by academic librarians doing a better job of introducing this exciting and challenging profession to a whole new generation, particularly a generation that thrives on just the kinds of changes and innovations that are so much a part of today's library job assignments. Don L. Bosseau and Susan K. Martin put it nicely: "We are failing in our duty to convey to pre-college students the nature of the excitement; the enjoyment of chasing an elusive fact; the pleasure of being part of many different people's studies and other pursuits; and the opportunity to participate in a national and international profession" (1995, 198).

What qualities are ideal for new librarians? While the literature on recruitment in libraries offers many answers to this question, key qualities include curiosity, flexibility, the ability and willingness to continue learning and to keep up with new technologies, and good people skills. In return, positions in academic libraries offer access to cutting edge technology, collegiality, continuous learning, challenges, constant stimulus of academe, the ability to make a difference, and the ability to influence the profession. By providing the flexibility, change, and opportunities that the new generation of librarians seeks, academic libraries will be able to recruit and retain them. A willingness to consider restructuring to re energize an individual's career is another strong motivator. Restructuring and retention go hand in hand, and that should be kept in mind. Recruitment does not end with signing on the dotted line.

Library residency programs (defined by ALISE as post-degree work experiences designed as entry-level programs for professionals who have recently received an MLS) have been in existence for several decades now. Yet research is just coming to light about not only how these structured programs contribute to the introduction of new professionals to the field of academic and/or research librarianship, but how they can address the critical issue of diversity in the profession as well. Since many large academic and research libraries do not routinely hire entry-level librarians, a residency program can orient and prepare the new professional at an accelerated pace in a way that is not generally available to traditional entry-level positions. Surveys have indicated that the majority of individuals who chose to enter residency programs may not have entered academic librarianship otherwise (Brewer 1997).

Academic libraries must find the most efficient and effective method to broadcast this exciting professional opportunity to young people who are growing up with computers in their homes, but who may never think about librarianship as a career because they don't come into face-to-face contact with a librarian. Many young people are convinced everything they need is "on the Web." The individuals behind the creation and updating of those Web sites, unfortunately, remain a mystery.

It is vital that academic librarians market the profession in a positive and exciting way. New and slick advertising campaigns with catchy slogans are not necessary. Nor is it necessary to focus on breaking the image of the old stereotype. The focus should be on the work of the profession. Discussions should take place at all levels throughout the professional associations, with library and information science educators, with campus administrators and student groups, and with those young people (all the way down to elementary school) who have not yet set their career paths in motion.

Effective recruitment, emphasizing the opportunities to affect education and to transform the image of academic librarians among youth, will bring new blood to the profession. This new generation of information professionals is interested in more than a steady job and paycheck. They seek a career chock-full of opportunities for change. "They want to be engaged in their work, and they want to be constantly stimulated" (Urgo 2000, 39). Academic librarianship is the right place for these new information professionals.

The New Career Contract

In *Developing Information Leaders: Harnessing the Talents of Generation X,* Marisa Urgo states that the key life motivators remain the same for Generation X (those born between 1966 and 1976) as for the previous generation or cohort (Baby Boomers): home, family, tranquillity. "The differences between generations do not lie in their substance but in their style" (2000, 8).

Generation X was the first group to grow up with computers as a part of their daily lives. Ms. Urgo's research shows that for this new generation of information professionals "change, even constant dramatic change, is better than no change at all." They are used to global interaction and culture, and they know how to exploit its opportunities and solve its challenges in new and imaginative ways that go beyond borders and boundaries.

As academic libraries look to replace the many librarians who will retire in the next ten years, it is necessary to understand what motivates and attracts this new generation of information-savvy professionals to academic libraries. This is an area ripe for research. While those currently working in academic libraries may understand the appealing concept of libraries as a continuous learning organization, it must be questioned whether this is enough to keep new recruits coming.

Douglas T. Hall and Jonathan E. Moss discuss the concept of the psychological contract of old (with the organization) versus the new career contract (with the self and one's work) in "The New Protean Career Contract: Helping Organizations and Employees Adapt" (1998, 22–36). This concept blends nicely with the personal and professional motives of new information technology professionals for the jobs they seek. If employers provide opportunities for continuous learning, the result will be the creation of continuous employability. This, in turn, may result in employee satisfaction, a form of job security, and employee retention. As employers, many academic library administrators state the need for flexibility in employees. It is just as important to demonstrate flexibility and adaptability in the organizational structure at large. By creating a path that provides continuous opportunities for learning, as well as for personal and professional growth, academic libraries will retain the informed, talented, and energetic individuals currently graduating from today's library and information science programs.

This new career contract may start out with creating a specific type of position that needs to be filled, but each institution has the ability to change the rules once the person is hired. That is to say, if an individual needs a career jump-start down the road, the institution must not sit by and passively allow that person to be recruited away. Career development is a responsibility of both the individual and the organization. Conversations between supervisors and individual librarians regarding opportunities, both within the institution and outside, are a necessary function of the career development process for academic librarians and an important aspect of performance management. Often, it is within an institution's ability to provide a change with very little cost or disruption to an existing department. A slight change in duties (such as the assignment of Web responsibilities) can make a world of difference to an ambitious librarian. Recruitment, restructuring, and retention are three concepts that must not be lost in today's competitive marketplace. They do not happen in isolation, but as a complete and dynamic phenomenon that must be addressed. For a more complete exploration of this three-pronged approach, see *Recruitment, Retention, and Restructuring: Human Resources in Academic Libraries* (ACRL Ad Hoc Task Force 2002).

Selection: A New Look at Screening for Tomorrow's Academic Librarians

Academic libraries typically employ search committees to ensure objectivity and buy-in from as broad a base of constituents as possible. Many libraries routinely invite a member of the teaching faculty to serve on such committees, which can have the added benefit of establishing good relations across campus after a search well done. Faculty members from outside the library (whether it be from a specific department or college, the provost's office, or a campus library committee) can bring a fresh, new approach to recruiting our own colleagues and can ensure that their departmental student or faculty concerns are being well represented and considered during the search process. Faculty members' participation can range from participating in only the campus interviews, to screening all applications, to participating in telephone and campus interviews, depending on their individual schedules. When the search is successfully completed, a faculty member may also be helpful in introducing the successful candidate to members of the teaching department or college—which can be a great way to start for the new librarian, particularly if the new hire is new to the profession and somewhat intimidated by the whole academic arena. Having a member of the teaching faculty on the search committee can build a positive rapport that will happily come back to haunt us when outside parties seek advice on how to conduct a good search. It is a win-win situation, and one well worth considering.

It should be mentioned that applicant pools, although slightly better as of this printing, are nowhere near the volume of five to ten years ago (100+ applications for one entry-level position). Perhaps a way to increase the number of viable candidates in these pools is to reconsider the application screening process. One way is to remind committee members that the best candidate is not always the most obvious candidate. Applications from individuals who have worked outside of academic or research libraries should not be discounted. A public or school librarian can be successful in an academic or research library. When screening applications, it is important to look for transferable skills and continued individual development and growth. Attention should be paid to the clues the applicant provides about what he or she is looking for, such as leadership opportunities.

Regarding the employment patterns and history of this new generation of librarians, statistics show that new MLIS graduates are getting slightly younger. Technology was as much a part of their lives growing up as were television and cars for Baby Boomers. "They do not want to see technology take over or replace library services, but they also do not want to work in an environment where technology is neglected, because it is the basic tool for service. Information managers should attempt to reach Generation X halfway. They should focus on the quality of service, on people, and on information opportunities" (Urgo 2000, 158).

Because these new information professionals actively seek out change and new opportunities to increase or upgrade their technology skills so that they can remain professionally engaged and competitive, they may relocate and change jobs more frequently than their predecessors did. Stability in employment history on a résumé should no longer necessarily be considered a good or expected thing.

The Role of the Interview:
The Most Critical Element

As so aptly stated by Douglas Birdsall, "the recruitment of librarians, properly conducted, can result in a ripple effect that creates an aura of professionalism in the library and among the campus community. Poorly done, the experience will leave bad feelings and an image of ineptitude which will be difficult to erase" (1991, 277). It is important for the library or organization to remember that the candidate is the number one priority during the interview.

If appropriate to the position, it may be helpful to extend an invitation to teaching faculty members to attend any open presentations or subject specialist meetings. Although some libraries contend that presentations are only of benefit to positions that involve formal instruction, others use presentations as a forum for additional staff members to see the candidates. This may provide a benefit for both the interview process and overall staff morale, as staff members want to lend their support to candidates as well as feel a part of the process. For support staff considering library school for themselves, seeing the expectations for interviews is an invaluable process. In addition, as librarians and professionals from all areas of the system are increasingly asked to conduct anything from informal workshops to teaching credit courses, the interview presentation has application for positions beyond formal instruction.

All staff members who participate in the interview process should provide the search committee with written comments regarding the presentation and/or interview process. Search committees consider much during the search process: the candidate's written application, their impressions from the interview itself, and comments from other library staff who participated in the interview. Quiet, reserved candidates should not necessarily be overlooked in favor of those who charm the staff. An effective search committee always considers the candidate's potential to do the job.

Interviews should be informative but at the same time should allow the candidate plenty of time to talk and ask questions. With experience, a human resources manager is able to anticipate most candidates' questions, depending on their level of experience (for example, department head and other senior-level candidates tend to want more information about retirement plans, although the new generation are pretty savvy about asking this, as well). When questions cannot be answered immediately, it is very important to respond to the candidate as soon as possible (preferably before he or she leaves campus).

Interviews are two-sided: The candidate is interviewing the library at the same time the library is interviewing the candidate. For both sides, being prepared and organized is the key. A candidate should leave the interview feeling he or she has learned as much as possible about the people and the organization, as well as about the actual job. The organization should have learned as much as possible about the candidate. A search that elicits information about the candidate in regard to the essential competencies (skills, knowledge, and attributes) for a particular position is a successful search.

Much has been written about "competency-based interviewing." According to CompQuick, a Web site maintained by MIT, "the basic principle of interviewing for competencies is this: *past behavior is the best predictor of future behavior*. In competency-based interviewing, candidates are asked about specific, actual past events in which he or she played an active role. Interviewers listen for evidence that the person demonstrated behaviors in those situations that are identical to or similar to the competencies the interviewer is looking for" (MIT 2000). Further refining and defining this principle for the library world, Joan Giesecke and Beth McNeil suggest interview questions that are designed to elicit the individual's analytical, problem-solving, and decision-making skills; communication skills; creativity and innovation; expertise and technical knowledge; flexibility and adaptability; interpersonal and group skills; leadership; organizational understanding and global thinking; ownership, accountability, and dependability; planning and organizational skills; resource management; and service attitude and user satisfaction (1999, 158–66).

Many of these intangibles are the very things that interviewers agonize over. A human resources manager's goal is to make sure the right candidate is placed in the right position. To do so, interview questions must be crafted ahead of time, for a more structured approach. Job-specific interviewing is more effective in identifying those individuals best suited to undertake the duties of a particular position successfully. As John Lehner stated, job-specific interviewing "offers, too, the prospect of increasing applicant satisfaction with the selection process, as well as increasing search committees' confidence in their recommendations" (1997, 203).

During the entire search process, from initial application to final decision, it is critical to stay in contact with applicants. All candidates have choices. Because the academic library search process is sometimes lengthy due to circumstances outside the control of the library, regular communication with candidates is essential. Search committees must stay on schedule and correspond with candidates in a timely and friendly manner. Candidates remember that personal attention whether they are the successful candidate or not. Word of mouth about a positive interview process can be a powerful tool for future vacancies, as well as the general reputation of the organization.

Conclusion

This chapter just skims the surface of the issue of recruitment and selection in academic libraries. Even when academic libraries have been fortunate enough to succeed in recruiting talented new professionals, the problem of retention still exists. Other chapters in this book address diversity and career development, both important factors relating to retention. In addition, ACRL's *Recruitment, Retention, and Restructuring: Human Resources in Academic Libraries* (ACRL Ad Hoc Task Force 2002) is an excellent example of collective and provocative brainstorming on these important topics within the profession. "The profession will die, not because people do not use libraries, but because people do not choose to be librarians" (Urgo 2000, 184). With successful recruitment strategies in place, librarians can influence others to choose librarianship as a profession.

Notes

1. *Baby Boomers* are commonly defined as those born between 1943 and 1964. See Kaufman (2002).

2. For more information on the "graying of the profession," see Chapter 3 in this volume.

References

Association of College and Research Libraries (ACRL). 2002–2003. *2002–2003 ACRL/ARL Recruitment Task Force.* Available: http://www.ala.org/acrl/dol-taskforce.html#recruit. (Accessed June 3, 2003).

Association of College and Research Libraries (ACRL) Ad Hoc Task Force on Recruitment & Retention Issues (a subcommittee of the Personnel Administrators and Staff Development Officers Discussion Group). 2002. *Recruitment, Retention, and Restructuring: Human Resources in Academic Libraries.* Chicago: Association of College & Research Libraries.

ARL Annual Salary Survey 2001–2002. 2002. Washington, DC: Association of Research Libraries.

Birdsall, Douglas G. 1991. "Recruiting Academic Librarians: How to Find and Hire the Best Candidates." *Journal of Academic Librarianship* 17, no. 5 (November): 276–83.

Bosseau, Don L., and Susan K. Martin. 1995. "The Accidental Profession: Seeking the Best and the Brightest." *Journal of Academic Librarianship* 21, no. 3 (May): 198–99.

Brewer, Julie. 1997. "Post-Master's Residency Programs: Enhancing the Development of New Professionals and Minority Recruitment in Academic and Research Libraries." *College & Research Libraries* 58 (November): 528–37.

Giesecke, Joan, and Beth McNeil. 1999. "Core Competencies and the Learning Organization." *Library Administration & Management* 13, no. 3 (Summer): 158–66.

Hall, Douglas T., and Jonathan E. Moss. 1998. "The New Protean Career Contract: Helping Organizations and Employees Adapt." *Organizational Dynamics* 26, no. 3 (Winter): 22–36.

Kaufman, Paula T. 2002. "Where Do the Next 'We' Come From? Recruiting, Retaining, and Developing Our Successors." *ARL Bimonthly Report 221*. Washington, DC: Association of Research Libraries.

Lehner, John A. 1997. "Reconsidering the Personnel Selection Practices of Academic Libraries." *Journal of Academic Librarianship* 23, no. 3 (May): 199–204.

Marcum, Deanna B. 2003. "CLIR Launches Program to Train Humanists in Libraries." *CLIR Issues* 32 (March/April): 3.

Massachusetts Institute of Technology (MIT). 2000, January. *CompQuick: Hiring for Competencies at MIT*. Available: http://web.mit.edu/personnel/irt/compquick/cq4.htm. (Accessed June 3, 2003).

Simmons-Welburn, Janice. 2000, May. "Changing Roles of Library Professionals." *SPEC Kit 256*. Association of Research Libraries, Office of Leadership and Management Services.

Urgo, Marisa. 2000. *Developing Information Leaders: Harnessing the Talents of Generation X*. London: Bowker-Saur.

5

Current Issues in Staff Development

Luisa R. Paster

Changes in the academic library workplace mirror those of other workplaces in the new millennium. Following the nature of the work, the organization of the institution is constantly shifting, requiring staff in all areas to perform a greater variety of tasks. The operations daily become more automated and more technical. The workforce becomes more diverse. The pace quickens. The budget tightens. And the tensions mount. Within this generic workplace framework, however, there are specific personnel considerations for academic libraries. As organizers, gatekeepers, and interpreters of knowledge, library staff must constantly become expert in new computer access technology and new research tools. Working in team-based organizations requires a new set of communication and coordination skills. Staff also need support for their enhanced roles of supervision and teaching. This period of constant culture change will require an integration of creative teaching and learning experiences throughout the library, for staff and patrons alike.

The issues and concepts identified in this chapter stand out from the author's own experience as Staff Development Librarian at Princeton University, from a perusal of many academic library Web sites, from the library literature, and from conversations with colleagues, as indicated in the references.

Keeping Current with Continuous Changes in Information Technology and with Information Itself

Obviously the most foundation-rattling development in academic libraries in recent years has been the explosion of the electronic information age. All systems have been automated, and libraries are now in the third generation of integrated systems for OPACS, acquisitions, cataloging, and circulation functions. More and more reference and research sources are digital, with frequent changes in acquisitions methods, searching techniques, and scope. Academic libraries must also react to the constantly changing nature of knowledge itself, particularly in the sciences. New fields of study are born and old ones are being merged in unexpected ways. Being computer literate is a given; the challenge now lies in staying current. The rapid turnover in daily tools requires a constant renewal of both technical knowledge and subject expertise.

Since 1999 Princeton Library's Social Sciences Reference Center has presented a series of informational sessions for the entire staff of SSRC. The goal is to keep staff current on new databases, to offer refreshers for subject areas with which they are not well acquainted, to provide tours of library units that affect their work, and to recognize the interdisciplinary nature of the social sciences. At each weekly meeting, one person is responsible for sharing with the others his or her expertise in a specific subject area, database, or other resource. Both librarians and staff members are involved in suggesting topics and making presentations. The program has been so successful that it has now expanded to the entire Public Services and Collection Development Department, and other staff development programs have been modeled on it.

Also in 1999 San Jose State University instituted a program to bring librarians in the social sciences and humanities up to date on the nature of science and its literature, both print and electronic, and on how to provide the best service to undergraduate and graduate students during those hours when a science reference librarian was not available. As at Princeton, the sessions were open to all full-time and adjunct librarians and to library staff who worked at reference points, and were led by in-house experts, in this case librarians in science fields, who shared their expertise. Evaluations of the program, called "Bootstrap Training," indicated that although the training was set up primarily to address the problem of keeping current with new databases, exposure to the basics of the science disciplines also proved valuable (Peterson and Kajiwara 1999).

Strengthening of Customer Service Orientation

The expectations of academic library users are rising due to the services provided by online booksellers and seemingly miraculous Internet search engines. Although academic libraries have always been service organizations, outreach must now be expanded. Academic libraries must offer new services; redefine the usual research services to accommodate new technologies; and adapt services to new constituencies, including returning students, and those with disabilities, with diverse ethnic backgrounds, and with different learning styles. This will require a culture change, from the passivity of waiting for patrons to arrive at the library with their questions to an assertive and enthusiastic promotion of library use both within and outside the library building itself.

At the University of Florida, "Delivering Good Customer Service" is offered quarterly as part of new staff orientation. The description states, "Giving good customer service will . . . increase your comfort with customers and consequently reduce stress. In this discussion workshop, we will identify basic steps in providing good customer service. We will also identify strategies for coping with difficult situations" (Di Trolio 2003).

For the past ten years The University of Delaware Library has been offering a staff program on understanding disabilities, focusing on communications skills and how to assist people. Neither medically nor legally oriented, its goal is to assist staff in being comfortable with the language required at a service point and in learning how to manage a service encounter. The program uses both video and handouts, which are updated for every session (Brewer 2002).

Since the first point of service for many library users is with student employees, training of this staff can make a noticeable difference. Bloomsburg University Library has developed an interactive instructional program to train student assistants to perform a wide variety of tasks including assisting patrons. Previous one-on-one training attempts were found to be inconsistent, inadequate for preparing students to serve patrons, and draining on supervisors' time. The Library engaged graduate students from the University's Institute of Interactive Technologies to develop an interactive program with four modules—basic customer service, the handling of periodicals, the handling of reserve materials, and the use of the OPAC—each with lesson content, assessment, and tracking of student achievement (Poole et al. 2001).

Development of a Teamwork Orientation

Propelled by shrinking budgets, decreases in the number of staff, and a blurring of the divisions between purely technical and purely public services tasks, the use of multifunctional teams is proliferating. The synergy of teamwork can compensate at least in part for the loss of staff, but it requires cross training and a rethinking of each staff member's role in the institution. This expansion of roles requires that attention be paid to information technology skills *plus* subject knowledge *plus* job-specific knowledge and skills all at the same time. Effective teamwork itself also requires some formal skill building, in addition to nurturing and encouragement from all levels of management.

At the University of Maryland organizational changes over the past four years have led to library-wide discussions of the key values of the Libraries and a statement of principles emphasizing teamwork, shared leadership, and the importance of learning and education for improved customer service. One principle summarizes the overall impetus: "Changing the culture in which we work by creating a shared vision and set of values that all can live by" (University of Maryland Libraries 2002). In response to these principles, a comprehensive "Learning Curriculum" was established, with ten components: Introduction to the Development of the Organization; Defining Customer Service; Measurement, Evaluation and Continuous Improvement for Planning and Decision Making; Development of Self, Teams and Workgroups; Exploring Leadership and Followership; Individual Improvement; Computer Skills; Library Basic Skills; Leadership Development; and Train-the-Trainers (University of Maryland University Libraries 2002).

Coordination of Technical Training and Finding the Expertise to Provide It to Staff

The need for ongoing, targeted, technical training for all levels of academic library staff is the headache that won't go away. No one medicine will do it all. Academic libraries need to identify appropriate competencies, perform needs assessments, establish classes, and provide one-on-one learning opportunities. And then take two aspirin and do it all again. But given the current funding situation, who will provide all this treatment? Is it the responsibility of the library? The college or university human resources department? The information technology department? Or perhaps outside vendors?

In any case it is clear that a designated individual or group is needed within the library to manage and promote the staff development program. Examples of individual positions include the Staff Development Librarian at Princeton, the Staff Development Officer at the University of Florida, and the Organizational & Staff Development Officer at Brown University. Advisory or implementation groups include the Library Education and Training Committee at Princeton, the Library Faculty/Staff Training and Development Committee at University of Notre Dame, and the Continuing Education Committee of the Academic Assembly of Librarians at Temple. Some institutions have both individuals and groups with different purviews and mandates.

To leverage funding most libraries join forces with the information technology department or the human resources department of the institution. This may allow for a greater array of training topics or a greater number of classes, but it may also require a relinquishing of control and of library specificity in the training. To create the Libraries, Computing and Technology Training Program (LCTTP), the Michigan State University Libraries have joined with Administrative Information Services, the Computer Laboratory, the Instructional Media Center, and Broadcasting Services. The program provides hands-on learning courses taught by professional instructors in a wide array of computer topics. Fees are charged, but an automatic Fee Waiver Program is available for faculty and academic staff for most classes (Michigan State University 2003).

Cornell University has devised a Colleague to Colleague program in which the training budget is allocated to send selected staff to advanced training programs outside the university, with the understanding that they will return to teach a beginning level class either on the same topic or on a different topic. By using the money on the advanced training instead of the beginners, the overall skill level of the staff is constantly being raised. The program has served also to create a culture of sharing, with staff members offering to provide training (Bryan 2002).

Support for New and Experienced Supervisors

Most librarians do not enter the profession with a management goal in mind, yet many end up in supervisory roles that consume much of their time and energy. As the organization reinvents itself, supervisors are asked to introduce new concepts to staff, use teamwork models, rethink performance appraisal schemes, and find ways to make do with reduced budgets. They need support both in the form of skills building and individual coaching. Informal support can be achieved internally with brown bag lunches, mentoring plans, and informational sessions, but formal supervisory training is usually supplied either from college or university sources or by outside vendors.

The University of Tennessee offers several programs for supervisors. One program is called SOAR, "Supervisors: The Organization, Achievement, and Responsibilities." The program includes a prerequisite course, "Effective Supervisory Practices" (ESP), followed by at least five SOAR electives. Another program, "SuperVision 20/20," is divided into three areas: Personnel Policies and Procedures, Fiscal Policies and Procedures, and Skills of Leadership and Management, each with specific class requirements. In addition there is a core class called "Leading at UT." Both these programs, as well as many others, are advertised on the Library Training Web page (Mack 2003).

Support for the Increased Teaching
Role of Academic Librarians

The new emphasis on information literacy has resulted in a greater integration of librarians into the teaching function of the academic institution. Traditional visits to classrooms to discuss research sources now include not only the classic paper sources but also electronic sources and the fine art of evaluating Internet sources. Library Web sites often include lessons on how to do research. Librarians are being called upon to teach both faculty and students how to use the auxiliary computer applications for research: citation management tools, Web authoring tools, and presentation tools. More and more colleges and universities are offering classes conducted completely or primarily online. Reaching students via distance learning requires a new panoply of teaching skills, in addition to considerable Web skills and knowledge of Internet communications technology.

This expanded educational role requires excellent teaching skills, including assessment of needs, lesson planning, presentation, and evaluation. Even for library staff who have teaching credentials and/or experience, new ways of learning require a renewal of teaching skills using interactive and technology-based methods. The Association of Research Libraries (ARL) has added to their Web site an extensive Training Skills Support Site, to assist both staff development librarians and all library staff who provide training (ACRL 2002).

According to Judy Peacock, Information Literacy Coordinator of The Queensland University of Technology (QUT):

> Although academic libraries have already established a 'training role' in universities, substantial technological, pedagogical and cultural changes occurring within the higher education sector now demand that reference librarians become educators. This complex role demands more than sound pedagogical knowledge, advanced teaching skills and an ability to develop, deliver and facilitate effective learning experiences. It also requires that the teaching librarian functions as an educational professional; that is, as one who can engage in educational debate and decision-making processes, influence policy, forge strategic alliances and demonstrate diplomatic sensitivity. (2001, 39)

To this end, in June and July 2000, the QUT Library participated in a local adaptation of the EduLib program, which was originally developed in the United Kingdom. (More information is available from the EduLib Web site at http://www.tay.ac.uk/edulib/index.html.) The series, which was mandatory for all teaching librarians, comprised eight workshop sessions of three hours' duration conducted over consecutive weeks on the following topics: understanding learning, the nature of teaching and teaching methods, working with diversity, evaluation of teaching and learning, developing an effective teaching portfolio, planning a T&L event, making presentations and planning/critiquing, and teaching practice. Based on the EduLib experience, the Library is working on a new Professional Information Literacy Development Model adapted to the QUT Library context (Peacock 2001).

Staff Development for Retention and Morale

The demographics of academic libraries are well documented and ominous. Changes in the labor market and the continued low unemployment rate mean that libraries are competing for qualified candidates not only with each other but also with other industries. The Baby Boomer bulge of experienced librarians continues to march toward retirement. To position itself as an attractive workplace choice, the academic library can capitalize on the educational mission of the institution by evolving into an environment that promotes and rewards staff learning. Tom

Cetwinski, Training Coordinator of the University of Georgia Libraries, reminds us that "Entry level positions are often accepted for what can be learned, in what skill one can become proficient. We look at such positions as apprenticeships. Isn't that how most of us became librarians?" (Cetwiski 2000).

He discusses three forms of learning: orientation, where new staff are welcomed into the culture of the organization and important first impressions are created; traditional classroom or workshop training, where the learning needs of a group are addressed; and targeted one-on-one learning situations such as personalized learning plans and mentoring, where each individual is made to feel a valued part of the organization. Support for education received outside the institution, such as college or university classes or pursuit of graduate degrees in library science, also allows both professional and support staff to fulfill their desire for growth while retaining their jobs in the institution.

Auburn University Libraries are addressing the retention and morale issue with a creative "Career Ladder" for long-term nonprofessional staff. With the active support of the dean and funding from the university, staff can apply for promotions by proving their competence in their current positions and participating in a series of required and elective courses. Each course has a proficiency test, which is euphemistically designated as a "learning celebration", to emphasize the educational aspect and the role of the supervisor as career guidance counselor (Ransel 2002).

Providing Individualized Opportunities by Integrating Learning into the Culture of the Organization

Despite the enormous planning and time investment they require, the massive one-time technical training efforts related to the introduction of a new library-wide procedure or automation system are easier to produce than the continuous training efforts required to keep staff current, to improve skills, and to change institutional culture. These latter efforts require constant renewal, flexibility, individual tailoring for diverse learning styles, and timing that provides the information or skill just when the learner needs it.

For this to occur, there must be an ambience of learning in the organization—a culture where formal and informal learning takes place every day, not just as a special event. Active support from the library director, including adequate funding, translates into support from department heads and ultimately from supervisors of work units. Where this occurs, it becomes clear that all members of the organization are both learners and teachers.

Academic libraries have found various creative ways to create a culture of learning. The University of Delaware Library uses a self-paced preservation training kit, including a manual with general information on how to handle different media, a video or two, and a quiz at the end. Aimed at new employees or student assistants, the program is approximately one hour long (Brewer 2002). The University of Maryland Library offers extensive online handouts, including tutorials, for classes in HTML, Excel, and PhotoShop (2003).

Yale provides an extensive "Learning Plan" program centered on a workbook where individual staff members integrate their personal learning goals with the library's mission, perform self-assessments to ascertain which competencies need development, reflect on their preferred learning styles, plan a continuum of appropriate learning activities, and discuss with their supervisor how best to attain the stated goals. The effort is supported by a Web site listing formal classes offered by the university, a resource library of books and multimedia, and links to online resources (Reynolds 2003).

Conclusion and Additional Resources

Over the past seven or eight years the need for library staff development has become so pressing that new positions have been established and current positions have been diverted partially or wholly to this end. Expenditures have also increased. According to statistics gathered by the ALA Office for Human Resource Development and Recruitment, expenditures for staff development and training as percentage of total payroll in 2001 were as follows: 1.26 percent for two-year colleges, 1.53 percent for four-year colleges, and 1.35 percent for universities (Lynch 2001). The figures still do not yet match industry norms, however. The American Society for Training and Development reports that American businesses spent an average of 1.8 percent of payroll on training in 1999 and projected an average 28 percent increase for 2000 (Lynch 2001).

Important recent documents for practitioners are the ARL SPEC Kit 224, "Staff Training and Development" (June 1997), and Kit 270, "Core Competencies" (October 2002). In May 2002, Carissa Pilotti, a Staff Development Intern at Cornell, produced a study based on telephone or e-mail interviews with thirteen of the top twenty ranked research libraries on topics such as orientation programs for new staff, technical training, personal interest classes, and staff development task forces (Pilotti 2002.)

The ARL Leadership Committee has also been considering staff development programs and how to identify best practices in this area. Rather than looking at budgetary and organizational inputs, which differ from institution to institution, the committee chose instead to analyze and delineate the factors that define excellence. These factors, described more fully with examples on their Web page, are a coherent curriculum, staff dedicated to the program coordination, target groups identified for training, program assessment and evaluation, resources, partnerships, and administrative commitment (ARL Research Library and Management Committee 2003). Other means of sharing and promoting staff development are offered by the Personnel Administrators and Staff Development Officers Discussion Group of ACRL, the LAMA Human Resources Section Staff Development Committee, and the Continuing Library Education and Networking Exchange Round Table (CLENERT) of ALA.

It appears that staff development is becoming an integral and appreciated component of the academic library organization. Institutions are experimenting with new learning techniques, new models of cooperation, and new ways to support the changing roles of librarians and library staff, and the ongoing cultural change of today's and tomorrow's academic libraries.

References

Association of Research Libraries (ACRL). 2002. *OLMS Training Skills Support Site*. Available: http://www.arl.org/training/ilcso/index.html. (Accessed October 22, 2003).

ARL Research Library and Management Committee. 2003. *Library Staff Development Programs: Key Components*. Association of Research Libraries.Available: http://www.arl.org/olms/staffdev/key_components. html. (Accessed October 22, 2003).

Brewer, Julie. 2002. Telephone conversation, December 9.

Bryan, Linda. 2002. Telephone conversation, December 4.

Cetwinski, Tom. 2000. "Using Training for Recruitment and Retention." *Georgia Library Quarterly* 37, no. 1: 5–10.

Di Trolio, Trudi. 2003. *Workplace Skills Series*. University of Florida George A. Smathers Libraries. Available: http://www.uflib.ufl.edu/ pers/training/Traininginfo3.htm. (Accessed October 22, 2003).

Lynch, Mary Jo. 2001. *Spending on Staff Development (2001)*. ALA Office for Human Resource Development and Recruitment. Available: http://www.ala.org/Content/NavigationMenu/Our_Association/Offices/ Human_Resource_Development_and_Recruitment/Library_ Employment_Resources/Spending_on_Staff_Development_(2001). htm. (Accessed January 2, 2003).

Mack, Thura. 2003. *Library Training*. University of Tennessee Libraries. Available: http://www.lib.utk.edu/~training/LibraryTraining/Training. html. (Accessed January 2, 2003).

Michigan State University. 2003. *Libraries, Computing and Technology Training Program*. Available: http://www.train.msu.edu/. (Accessed October 22, 2003).

Peacock, Judith. 2001. "Teaching Skills for Teaching Librarians: Postcards from the Edge of the Educational Paradigm." *Australian Academic & Research Libraries* 32, no. 1: 26–42.

Peterson, Christina, and Sandra Kajiwara. 1999. "Scientific Literacy Skills for Non-Science Librarians: Bootstrap Training." *Issues in Science and Technology Librarianship*. Fall Available: http://www.library. ucsb.edu/istl/99-fall/article3.html. (Accessed November 6, 2002).

Pilotti, Carissa M. 2002, May 31. "Benchmarking Staff Development Practices in ARL Libraries." Unpublished essay.

Poole, Erik, Frank Grieco, Heather Derck, and Tom Socash. 2001. "Training Library Student Assistants: Bloomsburg University's Interactive Instructional Program." *College & Research Libraries News* 62, no. 5: 537–38.

Ransel, Kerry. 2002. Telephone conversation. November 15.

Ransel, Kerry. n.d. *Information about Auburn University Libraries' Career Ladder Program*. Auburn University Libraries. Available: http://www.lib.auburn.edu/dean/career/. (Accessed October 22, 2003).

Reynolds, Katherine. 2002. Telephone conversation, December 11.

Reynolds, Katherine. 2003. *The Learning Plan*. Yale University Library. Available: http://www.library.yale.edu/training/stod/learningplan.html. (Accessed October 22, 2003).

University of Maryland Libraries. 2002. *The Learning Curriculum: A Comprehensive Learning Plan*. ARL Research Library and Management Committee. Available: http://www.arl.org/olms/staffdev/maryland. html. (Accessed January 2, 2003).

University of Maryland Libraries. 2003. *Staff Learning and Development: Computer Training Handouts*. Available: http://www.lib.umd.edu/ groups/learning/handouts.html. (Accessed October 22, 2003).

6

Assisting Employees

Julie Brewer

Managing employees with personal problems is the most difficult part of personnel administration. Drug and alcohol dependencies or episodic mental health concerns can disrupt an employee's performance and potentially threaten his or her employment. Health problems, accidents, and family crises, although temporary, can be overwhelming. Workplace conflicts and stresses are also disabling. Left unresolved, personal problems will naturally affect workplace productivity and morale.

Library human resource managers often feel unprepared to assist employees struggling with problems at home and work. Fortunately, many colleges and universities provide employee assistance programs (EAPs) to assist both employees and supervisors in managing these situations. Campus EAPs provide access to a network of community referral resources and counseling services to employees, as well as education and support to their supervisors. EAP professionals are valuable resources in helping employees resolve problems and improve productivity. This chapter discusses how library human resources managers can work effectively with EAP professionals to manage crises, improve workplace productivity and morale, and help employees balance their lives at home and work.

Employee Assistance Programs (EAPs)

The Employee Assistance Professional Association defines an Employee Assistance Program (EAP) as "a worksite-based program designed to assist in the identification and resolution of productivity problems associated with employees impaired by personal concerns, including, but not limited to, health, marital, family, financial, alcohol, drug, legal, emotional, stress, or other personal concerns which may adversely affect employee job performance" (1998, v). The intent of EAP programs is to help employees resolve stresses and conflicts and become more productive. Counseling and educational services can help employees deal with problems at home and work before they become disabling. Proactive organizations encourage employees to seek assistance and education before minor stresses become major problems.

Early forms of workplace assistance programs originated in the private sector in the 1940s to help employees struggling with drug or alcohol problems (Bickerton 1990, 35). Since then, the scope of EAP programs has expanded to address a variety of other employee problems. A survey of employee assistance professionals found that the most prevalent problems addressed were family issues (25 percent), stress (23 percent), depression (21 percent), alcoholism (14 percent), workplace/job conflict (9 percent), and drug abuse (2 percent) (Employee Assistance Professional Association 1996).

The first EAPs in higher education began in the 1970s. By 1989 there were approximately 150 EAPs in colleges and universities to meet the needs of faculty and staff (Lew and Ashbaugh 1992, 34). A small sample of liberal arts colleges, taken in 1996, found approximately half had campus EAPs (Pogue 1997, 21). Presumably, the number of EAPs has continued to increase, at least in larger academic institutions, as has been the trend in the private sector. According to the U.S. Bureau of Labor Statistics, 61 percent of workers at companies with 100 or more employees were covered by some sort of EAP in 1997. Fourteen percent of workers in smaller companies were covered in 1997 (*Statistical Abstract* 2001, 407).

EAP services may be provided as part of the campus human resources unit, by an external contractor, by the state department of personnel services, or by various combinations of these resources. Services may be provided on-campus, off-site, via the telephone, or on the Internet. The levels of service also vary from institution to institution. EAP services are generally offered free of charge to employees. Some college, university, and state personnel systems extend services to family members as well. In some cases the number of free counseling sessions may be limited or access may be restricted to supervisory referrals.

Campus EAP programs typically provide short-term counseling sessions, usually limited to fewer than a dozen meetings. Employees needing additional sessions or specialized services that go beyond immediate problem solving to maintaining job performance may be referred to other health care professionals. As referral agents, EAP professionals can advocate employee interests or help employees negotiate the complex array of social, legal, financial, and health care services. This assistance and support is particularly important at a time when employees are most stressed and least able to manage on their own.

Educational services such as parenting classes; alcohol support groups; and workshops on stress management, downsizing, and diversity may also be part of progressive campus EAP programs. EAP professionals can customize educational programs for library needs and may serve as consultants for specific departmental concerns. They often play a key role in campus training sessions on topics such as sexual harassment and violence in the workplace.

Managing Crises

EAP professionals are most valuable in crisis situations. They can be called on to assist when a group of employees experiences a trauma such as the death of a colleague or an act of violence in the workplace. EAP counselors can provide on-site grief counseling to coworkers who are emotionally affected. Even employees who are not directly involved in an incident may need assistance to feel secure at work. The widespread tragedies of September 11, 2001, demonstrated the importance of workplace EAPs. The use of EAP services increased dramatically, especially in the New York area, following the attacks (Prince 2002, 14).

Personal tragedies such as a sudden death in the family or the loss of a home to flood or fire are individual crises that may unexpectedly take employees away from work. The library human resources manager should refer the employee to the campus EAP as soon as possible. The manager should be prepared to describe the types of EAP services that may be useful in a given situation and provide an EAP brochure or business card to the employee. EAP professionals can help connect the employee to community resources to begin recovery and offer counseling services, if needed.

An employee experiencing severe stress or personal trauma cannot be expected to function effectively at work. EAP professionals can help assess whether the employee is able to continue work or would benefit from leave of absence. What the employee needs most at this point is empathy, understanding, and assurances that he or she does not need to worry about work on top of other personal challenges.

The library human resources manager should be prepared to give the employee information on available vacation and sick leave and explain provisions of the Family Medical Leave Act, if appropriate. The employee is likely to feel overwhelmed and may want to abruptly change employment status or work responsibilities to reduce stress. The employee needs to be reassured that the situation is temporary. The library human resources manager should work with the supervisor to identify what accommodations can be made to temporarily lighten the workload, reduce work hours, and shift job assignments, if possible. Since individual crises are very different, there is no standard formula to determine how much time away from work an employee may need. It's best to err on the side of being as generous and flexible as possible. Good employees do not abuse time off and generally want to return to work as soon as possible, both for financial reasons and to restore some order to their lives (Cohen 2001, 64).

While an employee is away from work, an EAP professional may act as an intermediary between the employee and the library. This is an important role when the employee is receiving mental health treatment or other assistance that may be sensitive. In many cases, the EAP professional will need to be an advocate for the employee to ensure that he or she is receiving adequate care. Employees who are experiencing trauma often lack the emotional resources to gather information and assert their needs.

EAP professionals can assist supervisors by providing information on how best to support the employee when he or she returns to work. They can clarify what kind of information may be provided to coworkers. They can assess the employee's condition and recommend whether he or she is able to return to work full-time or part-time and how soon. In medical situations, the conditions for returning to work may be dictated by a health care provider. The library human resources manager should work with the EAP professional to develop a transition plan for the employee's return to work.

Whether or not an EAP professional is involved, the library human resources manager is responsible for monitoring the employee's absence. The human resources manager may contact the employee directly or periodically check in with the EAP professional to understand the employee's progress. It is important to balance the needs of the library while providing assistance to the employee. Asserting workplace needs while trying to respect privacy and show concern for the employee requires great sensitivity and care.

Performance Management

Fortunately, most employee problems are less acute and do not require a significant amount of time away from work. Poor attendance and deteriorating productivity may indicate an employee is having trouble coping with a personal problem. Some employees readily volunteer personal information about their situation, providing a natural opportunity for the supervisor to make an informal referral to the campus EAP. Having access to a campus EAP allows the supervisor to be supportive and empathetic without becoming inappropriately drawn in to the employee's personal situation. A campus EAP allows the supervisor and employee to focus on job performance with the assurance that there are professional resources available for addressing personal concerns.

When performance problems persist, supervisors may need to initiate progressive performance management interventions. Many employees choose not to discuss personal matters with their supervisor. Others may deny or disagree that there is a performance problem. Although it is not appropriate to ask employees about personal matters, it is important to inform employees that the campus EAP provides confidential services to assist with performance problems.

If the supervisor does not observe improvements after an initial performance discussion and EAP referral, he or she may then document the concern in writing with a written referral to the EAP. The memorandum should describe the specific performance concern and how it affects the library. It should restate performance expectations and offer strategies on how to make improvements. Meeting with a campus EAP professional can be identified as a strategy for improving performance. References to personal circumstances should not be put in writing. The library human resources manager should work with the supervisor in drafting a written EAP referral and participate in the performance meeting with the employee.

During the performance meeting, the library human resources manager should describe EAP services and provide information on how to contact the EAP office. The manager can reinforce this information by giving the employee an EAP brochure or business card. The manager should express confidence that the employee is capable of meeting performance expectations. The tone of the meeting should be positive and emphasize that the EAP referral is a developmental opportunity rather than punitive. Most employees follow through on a written EAP referral. Even the most reluctant employees generally find some benefit to an EAP consultation.

If an employee is in serious jeopardy of losing his or her position, the EAP referral may be mandatory. The written referral may state that meeting with a campus EAP professional is a condition for continuing employment. This is a serious disciplinary matter that requires prior approval from the campus labor relations office. It also requires that the supervisor and library are willing to terminate the employee if he or she chooses not to comply. However, these instances are rare.

The library human resources manager can help the employee get appropriate services by actively communicating with the EAP office when making a referral. Employees are sometimes confused or so stressed that they do not effectively present their needs. The library human resources manager should give the EAP professional specific details about the employee's job responsibilities and performance expectations since EAP professionals do not know the requirements and priorities of every position. Most important, the human resources manager should express concern for the employee and interest in the employee's continued employment. EAP professionals are most effective when the library human resources manager and supervisor actively support the employee rather than send the employee to be "fixed."

EAP referrals demonstrate the library's interest in assisting employees with performance problems. A record of the services and accommodations provided shows that the library has made a good faith effort to assist an employee. Good documentation is essential to effectively manage performance and will work in the library's favor in the event that an employee pursues legal action (Ryan 1997, 6).

EAP professionals often assist employees with disabilities. Library human resources managers may rely on the EAP office to coordinate benefits, labor relations, and other campus services needed to help with disability issues. EAP assessments may identify previously undiagnosed learning disabilities when employees struggle with specific job responsibilities. EAP professionals can provide advice on documentation and record keeping, and counsel how far to pursue assistance, ADA accommodations, and rehabilitation.

Services and assistance provided by EAP reduce the traditional adversarial relationship between employees and employers. The EAP provides a forum for communication and conflict resolution. Employees who feel they have been treated well and received assistance are less likely to pursue legal action. They are also more likely to continue employment and be productive. Studies at the University of Michigan indicate that employees who use campus EAP services have higher retention rates and use less sick time than other employees (Bruhnsen 1994, 11). Improved retention and reduced use of sick leave translate into cost savings for the library.

Confidentiality

The reputation of an EAP rests on how well it protects private information. Employees often worry that their jobs may be endangered if their personal problems become known, so confidentiality is a primary concern for employees who use EAP services. EAPs provide a safe forum for handling sensitive personal information and resolving problems outside the immediate work environment, especially for those whose health care plan does not provide coverage for mental health services.

However, confidentiality requirements can make it difficult to communicate with an employee using EAP services. When referring an employee to the EAP office, the library human resources manager should clarify what type of information will be shared with EAP professionals and what type of information EAP professionals can share with the supervisor. The library human resources manager should review the EAP policy on confidentiality and use of work time for appointments with the employee, as well as procedures for notifying the supervisor of planned time away from work. If communicating with an employee becomes a problem, the library human resources manager can arrange to meet with the employee and the EAP professional together.

When an employee is having difficulty managing problems at home or work, supervisors and coworkers are often left with the conflict of how to show compassion while respecting privacy. They may or may not know the details of the problem or whether the employee is getting assistance, depending on how much personal information the employee has shared. If the employee suddenly goes on leave or is unable to return to work, coworkers are often at a loss.

Supervisors and coworkers also have difficulty finding closure when an employee leaves employment with no explanation. Gossip and speculation can be very harmful. Coworkers can become mistrustful of their supervisor and the EAP. Library human resources managers need to acknowledge when an employee is not returning to work. They can state that they have little information because it was a private matter. They should assure coworkers that the EAP provides the best assistance possible. Coworkers should be left with confidence that the employee was treated well and that they will be too if they ever need assistance.

Because of confidentiality requirements, library human resources managers may only know of employees who use EAP services via supervisory referrals. Campus EAP utilization patterns show that employee groups use EAP services differently. Fewer faculty use EAPS services than nonfaculty. They contact the EAP more often as self-referrals than as supervisory referrals (Stoer-Scaggs 1999, 36). Employees in lower-paying positions use EAP services more frequently and have a higher rate of supervisory referrals.

These differences may be explained by income and work environment. Faculty have a great deal of autonomy, flexible work schedules, and relatively vague performance criteria. Low visibility and unstructured work environments make it more difficult for faculty supervisors to identify deteriorating performance. Library staff work in a more structured environment with more rigid schedules. Their performance and attendance problems are easier to measure.

Income also affects campus EAP utilization. Junior faculty use EAP services more than tenured faculty. This may be because of the high stress of achieving tenure and lower pay, which results in the selection of lower cost health plans that do not provide mental health coverage (Lew and Ashbaugh 1992, 36). Library staff may be more dependent on campus EAP services than library faculty.

Staff Awareness

Effective marketing of EAP services and programs will ensure that employee crises are addressed as quickly and efficiently as possible. In the ideal workplace, employees will be familiar with EAP services before a need arises and will seek assistance independently or with the encouragement of concerned coworkers. Self-referrals are characteristic of a successful campus EAP with a positive reputation.

The most frequently used methods of promoting staff awareness include new employee orientation, campus newsletters, posters, and employee health fairs (Pogue 1997, 32). Library human resources managers can assist in raising staff awareness by making campus EAP brochures available in staff areas and encouraging attendance at EAP workshops and lunchtime seminars, when possible. EAP professionals may also be invited periodically to library meetings to talk about programs and services or to provide education on specific topics such as stress management.

Information about campus EAP services should be targeted specifically to library supervisors. Supervisory training should include a copy of the EAP program policy, emphasize management support, explain the role of the supervisor in implementing the policy, and demonstrate how to integrate it into the supervisor's performance management responsibilities (Sonnenstuhl and Trice 1990, 18). This information is best assimilated as part of general supervisory training focusing on performance management skills (Rogers 1984, 247). To successfully refer an employee to the EAP, a supervisor must possess effective performance management skills to assess problems and intervene in the most supportive, constructive manner possible.

Special efforts should be made to help new supervisors and supervisors who are new to campus become familiar with EAP services and programs. New supervisors should be encouraged to work with the library human resources manager when making a referral. They may also schedule an informational meeting with an EAP professional before making a referral to understand what to expect and what to convey to the employee.

Work/Life Programs

In addition to traditional EAP services, many higher education employers offer work/life programs to assist employees. Services provided by work/life programs may include child care resource and referral, parent education and support groups, elder care support and education, campus mammography screening, and group mortgage programs. A report of the sixth annual College and University Work/Family Association (CUWFA) meeting in the *Chronicle of Higher Education* describes a sampling of work/life programs in large universities: Pennsylvania State University Work/Life Program counsels employees on alternate work arrangements and medical leave; the University of Michigan Family Care Resources Program helps individuals caring for elderly or disabled parents; New York University Office of Work-Life Services advises on adoption, transportation options, and home safety checks; and the University of Washington program provides lactation stations and a nanny-share network (Romano 2001, B12).

Work/life programs take a "life cycle" approach to the changing needs of employees from the time they enter the workforce as young, single people to the time of retirement. Work/life professionals function as internal consultants for employees in different life stages as well as for supervisors attempting to work with those employees. They work to help managers and supervisors understand that policies and practices that encourage flexibility are desired by men as well as women and needed by staff as well as faculty (De Pietro 1995, 30).

The Families and Work Institute reports that more than half of corporate EAPs provide work/life programs. They are found in larger companies with many work sites. These companies have a larger proportion of top executive positions filled by women or minorities and employ a larger percentage of women or part-time employees (Galinsky and Bond 1998, XII).

CUWFA estimates that approximately 30 campuses nationwide have clearly defined, viable work and family programs (De Pietro 1995, 30). Other institutions blend work/life services with other programs. A trend has been to merge these services with campus EAPs. The University of Texas at Houston merged its work/life and employee assistance programs in 1998. As a result, the utilization of the EAP jumped from 0.5 to 12 percent, and the use of the work/life program increased from 8 to more than 16 percent. The positive collaboration has reduced the stigma and attracted clients that had not previously used the services (Herlihy 2000, 25).

With the integration of work/life programs, the conceptual mode of EAP service delivery has evolved from a focus on the "troubled employee" to focus on employee strengths, empowerment, and work environment (Van Den Bergh 2000, 8). EAP professionals are now offering more prevention, health and wellness programs, community building, and organizational intervention. They provide a holistic approach that considers environmental factors that affect an employee's ability to cope and perform at work. This new emphasis on organizational ecology involves EAP professionals in downsizing initiatives as the economic climate changes, in diversity programming as more women and minorities enter the workforce, and in other organizational development initiatives. Future EAP and work/life initiatives will provide services, benefits, policies, and programs that allow employees to be optimally productive.

Conclusion

In the past few decades, EAPs have become essential campus resources. They are effective in guiding employees and their supervisors through crises and assisting with difficult performance management problems. Library human resources managers working with EAP professionals can prevent many employee problems from becoming overwhelming disruptions at work. As a result, academic libraries are able to retain valuable employees who otherwise may leave employment.

For a library human resources manager, there is nothing more valuable than having access to a well-managed, progressive EAP program. Knowing that employees will be cared for provides great assurance in stressful situations. Employees who benefit from EAP services generally appreciate the flexibility and compassion shown to them and become more loyal employees as a result. The movement to include work/life initiatives on campus further enhances the quality of life at work and contributes to a healthy, motivated workforce.

References

Bickerton, Richard L. 1990. "Employee Assistance: A History in Progress." *EAPA Digest* (November/December): 34–42, 83–84, 91.

Bruhnsen, Keith. 1994. "Michigan Study Shows EAP Clients Use Less Sick Leave, Stay Longer." *EAPA Exchange* (August): 11, 27.

Cohen, Chelle E. 2001. "When an Employee's Crisis Becomes HR's Problem." *Workforce* 80 (January): 64.

De Pietro, Leslie. 1995. "Campus Work and Family Programs." *CUPA Journal* 46, no. 3 (Fall): 29–33.

Employee Assistance Professional Association. 1996. *Employee Assistance Backgrounder.* Arlington, VA: EAPA.

Employee Assistance Professional Association. 1998. *EAPA Standards and Professional Guidelines for Employee Assistance Programs.* Arlington, VA: EAPA.

Galinsky, Ellen, and James T. Bond. 1998. *The Business Work-Life Study, 1998: A Sourcebook.* New York: Families and Work Institute.

Herlihy, Patricia. 2000. "EAPs and Work/Family Programs: Different Paths, Same Purpose?" *EAPA Exchange* 30, no. 5 (September): 24–26.

Lew, Aimee T., and Donald L. Ashbaugh. 1992. "Employee Assistance Programs in Higher Education." *CUPA Journal* 44, no. 1 (Winter): 33–37.

Pogue, Gregory. 1997. *Employee Assistance Programs on Liberal Arts Campuses.* New York: University Press of America.

Prince, Michael. 2002. "EAP Use Surges After 9/11." *Business Insurance* 36, no. 36 (September 9): 14.

Rogers, Duane E. 1984. "Training Isn't Training: Strategies for Orientation." In *Employee Assistance Programs in Higher Education,* 243–47. Edited by Richard W. Thoreson and Elizabeth P. Hosokawa. Springfield, IL: Charles C. Thomas.

Romano, Carlin. 2001. "Get a Life and a Career." *Chronicle of Higher Education* (March 13): B12.

Ryan, Katherine C. 1997. "Evaluate Your EAP." *CUPA Journal* 48 nos. 1/2 (Spring/Summer): 5–8.

Sonnenstuhl, William J., and Harrison M. Trice. 1990. *Strategies for Employee Assistance Programs: The Crucial Balance.* 2nd ed. Ithaca, NY: Cornell University, School of Industrial and Labor Relations, ILR Press.

Statistical Abstract of the United States 2001. 121st ed. 2001. Washington, DC: U.S. Dept. of Commerce, Bureau of the Census.

Stoer-Scaggs, Linda. 1999. "Employee Assistance Programs in Higher Education." In *The Employee Assistance Handbook,* 35–58. Edited by James M. Oher. New York: John Wiley.

Van Den Bergh, Nan. 2000. "Where Have We Been? . . . Where Are We Going?: Employee Assistance Practice in the 21st Century." *Employee Assistance Quarterly* 16, nos. 1/2: 1–13.

7

Managing Work Performance and Career Development

Beth McNeil

Managing and evaluating work performance, or performance management, is one of the most important aspects of human resources management in libraries. Performance management is a process or system that begins when a job or position is defined and ends when an employee leaves the position. Broader than traditional performance appraisal, performance management includes developing clear and concise job descriptions; hiring appropriate people; providing a thorough orientation, ongoing training, regular coaching and feedback, and a system for career development; and developing a system for reconsidering all of the above when an employee leaves a position, because an effective performance management system is based on an organization's long-term plans and strategic initiatives.

Colleges and universities often face two questions with regard to performance management systems: Do faculty and nonfaculty participate in the same system, and does the system focus on both individual performance and group/team performance? These issues apply to academic libraries as well, and for academic libraries where librarians have faculty rank, this first issue is especially important.

This chapter focuses on the performance evaluation and career development components of performance management for librarians and library staff. Other chapters in this book cover recruitment and selection, staff development, and compensation and benefits, all important aspects of overall performance management.

Performance Management

At the most basic level, steps for any performance appraisal system should include the following:

1. Determine what the job is (define the goals).

2. Establish a reasonable performance level (define the objectives in terms of quantity, quality, time spent).

3. Measure the actual performance (by first-hand observation, viewing completed work, reading employee's own report, etc.).

4. Compare the actual performance to the standards set. (Kroll 1983, 27).

Performance appraisal systems are a mechanism for feedback. They can be a basis for promotion, termination, and employment; can help guide other personnel in decision making; and can serve as a guide to career development. Some libraries are constrained by institutional policies as to how and when evaluations take place (Osif 2002, 47). Regardless of these constraints, however, administrators and human resources professionals may find valuable components in even the most inflexible performance evaluation system.

Identifying and Determining Effective Behaviors

The first step to managing performance is to develop a job description that spells out very clearly the expectations for the position. Job descriptions are the official statement of what an employee does or should do. Expectations should include those of the supervisor, the department, the library, and even, perhaps, the greater organization outside of the library (the university, the board of directors, etc.). The development and maintenance of current and accurate job descriptions is vital to the job analysis process. The job description is a written statement that describes the work that is to be done and the knowledge, skills, and abilities needed to perform the work. Job descriptions serve a variety of purposes. They introduce new employees or applicants to the job, provide basic documentation used in job analysis and compensation planning, set performance standards and help employees understand what is expected of them, provide a basis for setting goals and objectives, and identify and document essential job functions to ensure compliance with applicable laws and with other legal and workplace requirements (University of Nebraska 2001). The goal of a job description is to describe a position in sufficient detail so that the employee, supervisor, other staff members, and human resources staff will understand the work of any employee in that position.

Components of a Job Description

Job descriptions should include, in addition to required general information, a job summary, detailed list of duties and responsibilities, necessary qualifications, and, if pertinent, any physical requirements for the position. For librarians with faculty status or rank, job descriptions may also include expectations for research/creative activity and professional service. At a minimum, general information should include the name of the person who wrote the position description and when it was last updated. A summary of the position should state the role of the position and describe the purpose of the job. This brief statement will prove helpful for busy human resources professionals and other administrators who regularly review many position descriptions. The listing of duties and responsibilities should be detailed enough so that someone unfamiliar with the position could understand the tasks to be accomplished. Many position descriptions include the percentage of time devoted to each task, as well as an indication of whether the task is essential to the position. The use of clear, concise, and consistent language is very important for delineating duties and responsibilities, particularly when a task may be done by more than one employee. For employees completing the same task, supervisors should take care to use consistent wording to describe these tasks, even if the level of work and amount of time devoted to the task may vary between employees. Job descriptions are management tools that clarify work expectations, help employees understand their jobs, and can be used as a basis for performance evaluations.

Orientation and Training

Thorough orientation and training is invaluable. Without a clear understanding of policies and procedures, a new employee, or even a long-term employee moving into a new position, is not likely to meet early performance expectations. Good communication between employee and supervisor regarding performance objectives in terms of quantity, quality, and time spent, is paramount for employee success. Every supervisor should have a checklist of information to be covered when introducing a new employee to the unit, department, and organization. Early orientation activities include

- An introduction to colleagues in the unit or department,

- An orientation to policies and procedures and how to find them (This might be through distribution of a "new employee packet" or a thorough introduction to the library's staff Web site or library intranet), and

- A prearranged schedule for new employee to meet with pertinent people (Depending on the nature of the position these may include colleagues in other departments, unit heads, department chairs, and individuals outside the library).

Larger libraries may consider offering regularly scheduled general orientation sessions for new employees to gather, meet one another, and receive a general, library-wide orientation. A session of this sort might include

- A review of the organizational chart– (who does what and what services are provided by which unit),

- A review of major organizational documents (mission, vision, organizational goals for current year, etc.),

- A review of the library's service philosophy, and

- Small group exercises (relating to customer service issues).

While it is necessary for library staff at all levels to receive a thorough general orientation to the library, the library system, their unit or department, and their specific job, librarians with faculty positions will also need an orientation to the privileges and responsibilities that accompany faculty rank. The requirements for continuous appointment (sometimes referred to as tenure) and promotion may vary from library to library, and even an experienced librarian new to an organization may need significant orientation to the vagaries of the institution's tenure policies and procedures.

Performance: Evaluation, Assessment, or Appraisal?

Many definitions for performance evaluation, performance appraisal, performance assessment, and similar terms exist (Hodge 1983, 235; Kroll 1983, 27; Giesecke 1997, 24), but they tend to vary only slightly in their meanings. For the purposes of this chapter, all three terms refer to the same process: the formal assessment of an employee's job performance in relation to the duties and responsibilities of the employee's position, as detailed in the job or position description. As stated by Paul Kearns, "You can't manage what you don't measure. But don't just measure what you can. What gets measured gets done. A baseline and target performance measure should always be established" (2000, 5).

Various criteria have been suggested for use in developing, assessing, and applying a performance appraisal system. Stanley Hodge, in an article discussing the legal aspects of performance management, suggests the following criteria for application of performance appraisals:

1. Performance expected of employees is communicated and goals and objectives of the ratee's job are made clear in terms of behavior and the results to be achieved.

2. The ratee is advised of the purpose(s) of the appraisal.

3. At least two levels of supervisors review an appraisal before an evaluation is presented to an employee, particularly when it results in an "unsatisfactory" rating.

4. Persons completing the appraisal base their ratings on personal knowledge of the ratee's performance and contact with the ratee.

5. Problems that may be hampering job performance are discussed with the ratee.

6. An opportunity is provided for the evaluatee to voice opinions during the appraisal process.

7. Procedures exist for employees who disagree with any aspect of an evaluation to appeal to higher management or a review committee. (1983, 238)

Informal Assessment of Work Performance

Regular assessment of performance, through daily contact or weekly meetings, can be relatively informal. After a job description has been developed, regular meetings with an employee can help a supervisor to determine how well the employee is functioning in the position. Supervisor and employee can review the progress made and work completed since the last meeting. If additional assistance, training, or other support is needed, the supervisor can make appropriate plans. During a regular meeting or interaction, the supervisor and employee should review the work scheduled for the next period, adjust any goals or objectives as needed, and address any ongoing issues that either the employee or the supervisor brings to the meeting.

Feedback and coaching are most effective when the employee receives them at the time that an incident—either positive or negative—occurs. Small problems can be corrected before they turn into large ones, and successful behaviors or techniques can become regular routines. Immediate feedback helps the supervisor at annual evaluation time, as there should be no surprises for the employee in the annual evaluation.

Annual Performance Review

An effective performance evaluation or appraisal system is an ongoing process and often includes a formal evaluation of performance. Gedeon and Rubin, in their work on attribution theory and performance evaluation in academic libraries, list several purposes for performance evaluation, serving both the employee and the organization, including

- Providing a formal opportunity for supervisors to discuss performance with their subordinates;

- Helping the employee understand levels of expected performance;

- Providing feedback on the extent to which the employee is meeting performance expectations;

- Identifying areas of performance that need improvement;

- Recognizing outstanding performance;

- Providing information for human resources decisions such as promotion and tenure;

- Identifying structural or managerial problems, including quality of supervision and the efficacy of the system rewards and punishments; and

- Providing documentation for work references, or in case of challenges to employment decisions. (1999, 18)

Performance appraisal most typically takes place at an annual evaluation, although some libraries employ other methods as well. Performance evaluation is generally a formal and less frequent process and may include comprehensive evaluations, such as 360 degree or bottom-up evaluations, as well as other types of evaluation of performance. Regardless of method or process, performance measurement can be defined as "a conscious, objective assessment of the extent to which an individual is fulfilling or exceeding the requirements of their role, both in absolute and comparative terms" (Kearns 2000, 28). This assessment should be directly related to the duties and responsibilities outlined in the position description. Performance evaluation is based on a formal one-to-one meeting between the supervisor and a staff person. An appraisal helps to set objectives for the staff member for the coming year. These objectives should be based on the organization's goals, should be achievable within a year, should be agreed upon by manager and employee, and should be written down in an agreed upon format.

Benefits of Performance Evaluation

Organizational benefits of performance evaluation include readily available information for decisions on salaries and wages. Performance appraisal data can also help library administration to better make organizational structuring decisions, as well as alert it to previously untapped staff strengths and talents. "Performance appraisals help reduce uncertainty within the organization, and when combined with other programs may help to reduce externally related uncertainty as well" (Kroll 1983, 28). For the employee, performance appraisal at the most basic level provides feedback on how well he or she is performing in the current position. Additional benefits for the employee may include the shaping or development of plans for future career development within the current library or in other organizations.

Career Development

Not so long ago it was not unusual for a library worker to stay at the same library for his or her entire career. In some cases these individuals worked in the same position for many years, whereas others merely moved or advanced to new roles in the same organization. This is no longer the situation in most libraries. Today, continuous learning is essential for all library staff, whether or not they seek advancement. Due to reductions in funding, major changes in services offered, and a dramatic shift in the needs and desires of new generations of library workers, librarians and library staff are in need of career development opportunities to help them prepare for changes in their current positions, for advancement to future positions within their existing library or at another library, and even for positions outside the field of librarianship.

Thomas Wilding offers the following definition for career development: "the acquisition of knowledge and skills that eventually leads to the accrual of additional or different responsibilities and ultimately leads to the achievement of an individual's personal goals as a librarian" (1989, 899). Professional development, described by Wilding as "maintaining improving skills to keep up with the changing world around us" (1989, 899), and staff development, discussed in Chapter 5 in this book, are both related to career development. Whereas staff development is an organizational responsibility and professional development is a personal responsibility, career development is the responsibility of both the individual and the library organization. Kitty Smith suggests that responsibility for career development is shared also by professional associations and library educators (1995, 24). This suggestion is supported by the Library Career Pathways Task Force, of the 1st Congress on Professional Education. The Task Force was charged to review the means, methods, and expectations for entry into the library professions. The Task Force reviewed a policy statement approved by the ALA Council on June 30, 1970, and updated the policy to include a more current view of librarianship. The restatement of policy was adopted by consent by the ALA Council on January 23, 2002, at the Midwinter Association meeting. Of particular interest is the section of the policy on career development and continuous learning:

> Career development and continuous learning is the shared responsibility of the individual, the employer, formal education providers, and professional associations. Continuous learning is essential for all library and information studies personnel whether or not they seek advancement.

> Employers are responsible for providing training that supports the work of their organization. This can take the form of planned staff development activities or less formal activities such as committee assignments and special projects.

Employers are responsible for providing support for individual career development and continuous learning. Examples of support include release time, sabbaticals, tuition reimbursement, and mentoring programs. Such support is essential in hiring and retaining an excellent workforce.

Education providers are responsible for developing and making available learning opportunities that reflect the needs of the library and information studies profession. To address individual learning needs and styles, these must be available in multiple formats and in a variety of locations.

Professional associations are responsible for providing learning opportunities that meet the needs of their membership. These may take the form of workshops, conference programs, and articles in professional journals. Workshops and conference programs should be planned to ensure adherence to the best practice of adult learning theory.

For the individual, career development and continuous learning includes both formal and informal learning situations and need not be limited to library and information studies. In some cases, post-masters and doctoral programs may be appropriate. (ALA Policy 54.1 2002)

Past limiting factors for career development included rigidly defined position descriptions, detailed and highly structured job classification systems, lack of job openings at higher levels, and the inability to advance without changing jobs. These limitations led to low employee morale, resulting in either high turnover or a lack of initiative and interest on the part of continuing staff for learning new job skills, sometimes referred to as a "what's in it for me?" attitude.

Recent staffing trends in academic libraries are helping to decrease these limitations. These trends include a reduction in the number of librarians in some areas, with positions being either eliminated or moved to other areas. For example, some technical services positions are moving to public services, automation, or digital initiatives. As a result, support staff roles are expanding to include higher-level duties (Ransel 2002).

For support staff, these trends, combined with more flexible classification systems, are leading to increased possibilities for career development. Broadbanding, a compensation and classification system relatively new to academic institutions, allows staff to move into new duties and responsibilities without the former restrictions of highly structured job classification systems. Both staff members and organizations benefit: Staff have new, interesting duties and responsibilities, with the possibility of increased compensation, and organizations have much more flexibility to assign existing staff to activities to advance the ever-evolving work of the academic library.

Central to broadbanding programs is an emphasis on staff development and training. In the private sector, many companies utilizing broadbanding as a compensation/classification system create career management programs for staff. These programs help an employee to plan his or her career and develop the skills and competencies needed to assume greater responsibilities or move to a different position or level within the organization. Skill testing, values clarification exercises, guidance on training and educational programs, informal support groups, and mentoring arrangements are often part of the career management program. In 1994, the American Compensation Association, in conjunction with Hewitt Associates, surveyed 116 broadbanded companies. Although the survey revealed that employees and managers placed different levels of importance on career development/management, there was no question that career development was a significant factor in the success of the broadbanding implementation and in the success of the companies (Kahlc 2002, 2).

Career Development Process

Kitty Smith suggests that there are three essential steps in the career development process:

1. [A]n employee must assess [his or her] own goals and capabilities (internal needs assessment).

2. [M]anagers must work with employees to provide information and assistance in matching personal and organizational concerns.

3. [E]mployers and employees work together to develop an action plan for ownership of the process and responsibility for the results. (1995, 25)

Librarians and library staff share in the responsibility for their professional, and career, development. First, employees must determine what they want their careers to be. Working with the supervisor, each employee—whether librarian or library staff member—must assess his or her own skills and knowledge and acknowledge both strengths and weaknesses. The next step is the development of a plan to enhance or acquire the skills the employee will need to meet the career goal. The plan may include steps for development in the current position, as well as a plan for long-term career development. Agreement between supervisor and employee is necessary regarding the appropriate on-the-job training for the current position.

Supervisors should be prepared to design jobs that are challenging and interesting, to provide candid feedback on performance, to encourage learning at all times, and to alert staff members to job opportunities that offer development options, even when the opportunity may take the employee out of the unit or department.

Developing staff is crucial to organizational success. If library staff are to contribute to the best of their abilities to the library and the profession, they need to gain new knowledge and develop new skills and to share their knowledge and learning with others. Library leaders and managers need to support and encourage staff to apply these new skills in the workplace. Doing so helps to make learning an integral part of the responsibilities and activities of each employee.

Library administrators might consider the following questions when planning directions for career development for librarians and library staff:

- How will the needs, demands and expectations of our customers change?

- How will the librarian's workday change over the next five years?

- How will we co-operate and/or compete with each other and address the efforts of those outside the profession who also seek to provide information services?

- Will we remain a profession or will we become a group of highly specialized technocrats?

- How can we preserve and enhance the model of library practice? (Agha 2001, 400)

For organizations, steps to creating a career development program include creating awareness of the program; enlisting the support of managers; encouraging interested employees to consider their strengths, work preferences, development needs, and long- and short-term career goals; developing a shared awareness or understanding of goals; implementing a development plan; and following-up with a periodic review and assessment of the development plan (Gooding 1988, 113).

Transferable Skills

Possible broad career development areas for information professionals include visioning and planning skills, information handling skills using new technology, influencing and negotiating skills, creativity and learning, teamwork and leadership, change management skills, adding value to new services, forging alliances to provide innovative and effective services, and offering dynamic support services to enhance learning and research (Agha 2001, 401). Joan Giesecke suggests that the knowledge and skills needed today, which department chairs or unit heads should be helping librarians and supervisory staff develop, include (1) knowledge of the global environment, (2) knowledge of the organization, (3) knowledge of the information business, (4) basic management skills, (5) planning skills;,(6) interpersonal relationship skills, (7) communication skills, (8) skills at developing others, and (9) management abilities (2001, 48–49). For librarians seeking career changes, either at their current organization or through a move to a new position at a new organization, a plan for developing these areas is critical.

Motivation and Performance

Many factors motivate library staff, including working in an environment where difference is valued and new ideas welcomed, where risk taking is encouraged, and where the culture is one of cooperation rather than competition.

Performance appraisal, which includes frank and constructive feedback, positive reinforcement, and recognition of achievement, has for many years been considered a motivation tool for many employees (Kaehr 1990, 13; Lubans 1984, 15; Kearns 2000, 91). New generations of library staff are forcing libraries to look for new ways to motivate. The "Baby Boom" generation wants very much to excel, moving up in a challenging career path, while building a stellar career. Unsurprisingly, Baby Boomers are the generation that adopted the annual performance evaluation system. For Baby Boomers, performance appraisal or evaluation is a powerful motivator, for many of the reasons listed previously. As this group ages and new employees join libraries, however, new ways to motivate and reward upcoming generations of library employees must be found. Younger employees thrive on challenge, training, and new opportunities. For "Generation X" employees, motivations or rewards include freedom, balance in their lives, and transferable retirement packages. A long career at a single institution is not an expectation of many younger staff, and this may affect the factors, such as performance appraisal, that motivate their performance (Jurkiewicz 2000, 61). Attention to motivational factors for library workers of future generations will continue to be an important and necessary activity for human resources professionals.

Rewarding Performance

Human resources professionals have long held that performance evaluation and salary review should not be handled simultaneously (Kroll 1983, 32; Hilton 1978, 41). Due to the economic situation and funding problems for higher education today, for many colleges and universities, merit increases may be the only additional salary dollars available, if any money is available at all, and merit increases are typically tied to job performance. When available salary increases are very low or nonexistent, morale and subsequently employee performance may suffer. Although salary decisions are not necessarily made at the same time as performance evaluation, the two are linked. During periods with no salary increases, new ways must be found to reward and encourage employees.

For the new generations of library employees, salaries and wages may no longer be the most important reward. Employees in the Generation X group prefer balance in their lives, with time to "have a life," as well as transferable retirement plans. The even younger Millennial generation prefers tangible rewards they can use now, such as movie or event tickets. Millennials, or Generation Ys, feel rewarded when they can work in teams, participate in decision making, and have skill-building opportunities (Hays 1999). Academic libraries must find additional ways to reward excellent performance, or they run the risk of losing talented library staff.

Conclusion

Libraries should have in place regular, formal methods of performance evaluation or appraisal, which are understood and supported by supervisors at all levels in the organization, as part of the basic human resource functions (Gedeon and Rubin 1999, 18). Supervisors must know the duties and responsibilities of the position and schedule and conduct regular meetings and check-ins to monitor progress and track problems and concerns. Effective management of work performance includes both a thorough review of the past and a detailed, yet flexible, plan for the future. Consistent and fair management and evaluation of work performance is important for all positions, from library clerks, to librarians, to library administration.

Performance appraisal can be difficult, particularly for new supervisors (Giesecke 1997, 24). Performance appraisal can be challenging, as well, for experienced supervisors, particularly in cases of underperformance of long-term employees. Regardless of situational differences, performance measures should be easily expressed and simple to understand. They should be meaningful in size and importance. Both supervisor and employee should agree upon and accept the performance measures, and performance measures should motivate employees to be high performers. A supervisor's goal is to work with individual staff members to achieve good performance, in terms of both quantity and quality. This process requires time, and it can be tempting to push it aside for other pressing activities. An effective performance appraisal, arguably one of the more important components of a performance management system, takes into account organizational policy and legal requirements, and includes job standards and criteria, a career development plan, and evaluator judgment and training. For academic libraries, the benefits of an effective performance management system and career development process include improved recruitment and retention, greater flexibility for individuals and within group work, and improved productivity. Career development plans and effective performance appraisal systems allow both library staff and supervisors to best meet the changing staffing needs of academic libraries.

References

Abosch, K. S., and J. S. Hand. 1998. *Life with Broadbands*. Scottsdale, AZ: American Compensation Association.

Agha, Syed S. 2001. "Professional Development: Specialization or Hybridization." *Library Review* 50, nos. 7/8: 400–2.

ALA Policy 54.1. 2002. (Restatement of ALA Policy 54.1 was adopted by consent by the ALA Council on January 23, 2002, at the Midwinter meeting of the Association in New Orleans, LA.)

Gedeon, Julie A., and Richard E. Rubin. 1999. "Attribution Theory and Academic Library Performance Evaluation." *The Journal of Academic Librarianship* 25, no. 1: 18–25.

Giesecke, Joan. 1997. "Appraising Performance." In *Practical Help for New Supervisors,* 24–34. 3rd ed. Edited by Joan Giesecke. Chicago: ALA Editions.

Giesecke, Joan. 2001. *Practical Strategies for Library Managers.* Chicago: American Library Association.

Gooding, Lenn J. 1988. "Career Moves-for the Employee, for the Organization." *Personnel* 65 (April): 112–14.

Hays, Scott. 1999. "Generation Z and the Art of the Reward." *Workforce* 78, no. 11: 44–46.

Hilton, Robert C. 1978. "Performance Evaluation of Library Personnel." *Special Libraries* 69: 431.

Hodge, Stanley P. 1983. "Performance Appraisals: Developing a Sound Legal and Managerial System." *College & Research Libraries* 44: 235–44.

Jurkiewicz, Carole L. 2000. "Generation X and the Public Employee." *Public Personnel Management* 29, no. 1 (Spring): 55–74.

Kaehr, Robert E. 1990. "On My Mind. Performance Appraisal, Who Needs it?" *The Journal of Academic Librarianship* 16, no. 1: 35–36.

Kahle, Larry L. 2002, November. Internal report on enhanced staff development at the University of Nebraska-Lincoln Libraries.

Kearns, Paul. 2000. *Measuring and Managing Employee Performance: A Practical Manual to Maximize Organizational Performance Through People.* London: Pearson Education Limited.

Kroll, H. Rebecca. 1983. "Beyond Evaluation: Performance Appraisal as a Planning and Motivational Tool in Libraries." *The Journal of Academic Librarianship* 9, no. 1: 27–32.

Library Career Pathways Task Force, 1st Congress on Professional Education. n.d. *Library and Information Studies Education and Human Resource Utilization: A Statement of Policy Executive Summary.* Available: http://www.ala.org/hrdr/lepu.pdf. (Accessed March 15, 2000).

Lubans, John, Jr. 1984. "Performance Evaluation: Worth the Cost?" *North Carolina Libraries* 41 (Spring):15–18.

Osif, Bonnie. 2002. "Evaluation and Assessment, Part 1: Evaluation of Individuals." *Library Administration and Management* 16, no. 1: 44–48.

Ransel, Kerry. 2002. "Career Ladder Opportunities for Paraprofessional Library Staff at Auburn University Libraries." Presentation at ALA annual meeting, June 15, Atlanta, Georgia.

Smith, Kitty. 1995. "Career Development as a Remedy for Plateauing." *Library Administration and Management* 9, no. 1 (Winter): 23–26.

University of Nebraska. 2001, August. "NU Values Administration" (unpublished manuscript).

Wilding, Thomas. 1989. "Career and Staff Development: A Convergence." *College & Research Libraries News* 10 (November): 899–902.

8

Recent Labor Relations Activity and Academic Libraries

Lila Fredenburg

> There has been an explosion of student interest in labor issues.—
> Andrea Culver, full-time liaison to the student movement for Hotel Employees and Restaurant Union (Moberg 2002, 21)

Two dramatic and highly publicized movements occurring on university campuses may have a considerable impact on current labor relations in academic libraries: graduate student unionization and student involvement in Living Wage and similar campaigns. The election of John Sweeney to the presidency of the AFL-CIO in 1995 coincided with renewed efforts to involve communities in critical labor issues or grassroots organizing (Robinson 2000, 110). Efforts such as these are often referred to as community unionism or social movement unionism (Johnson 2000, 139). Union Summer, a labor internship program for college students, formed a significant part of that effort (Lewis 1996, A1).

Over the past several years, student-led, community unionist efforts have emerged on campuses in parallel forums: students in support of university workers and students in support of themselves as workers.

The growth of these activities and the media attention focused on them promise continued movement toward consolidation of efforts and activities among union-related causes and various collective bargaining units on university campuses. As a result, issues such as pay, automation, and job preservation in academic libraries will receive attention, publicity, and pressure from such groups. Living wage campaigns on campuses initially focused on the very lowest paid employees such as part-timers, janitors, and groundskeepers (Moberg 2002, 21). However, as demands of those groups are met, the emphasis will (and in some cases already has) shift to library workers as a historically low-paid group (Milgram 2001). Attentive library administrators must seek to meet those concerns that might otherwise find an outlet in community unionism (Wallack 2002). Libraries that have not been unionized to date could be likely targets for community union efforts.

Students in Support of Other Workers

The student movements focusing on workers' rights have quickly spread across university campuses of varying sizes and missions (Krueger 2001). Student organizations initially focused their efforts on the abuses of globalization, with campaigns against sweatshops that demanded that universities cease using targeted suppliers for university-logo clothing (Zahra 1999). But that effort soon expanded. In 2001, living wage campaigns (a grassroots movement begun in local communities, which demands that local governments and merchants commit to paying workers a living wage) were active at twenty-one universities (Manners 2001, 16). Students soon recognized the community as their schools and demanded the administration pay living wages to all university workers (Krueger 2001). By mid-2002, Living Wage campaigns on campuses had grown to over thirty-four (ACORN n.d.) and the list of universities with anti-sweatshop organizations numbered over 200 (Bernstein 1999, 86). An acknowledged alliance with organized labor has accompanied these movements. The Harvard student sit-ins, for instance, had major and visible support from local and national unions (Tilly 2001).

The dining hall workers at Harvard, who were in the midst of bargaining their own labor agreement, listed amnesty for the students as one of their demands. AFL-CIO lawyers helped draft the students' final agreement with the university (Manners 2001, 16). The same type of support is visible on other campuses as well.

Students Organizing Themselves

Graduate assistants took their cue from adjunct faculty, who engaged in successful unionization efforts after years of frustration with low pay and lack of recognition in the late 1990s at Columbia College (Leatherman 1998, A16) and Roosevelt University (Schneider 1998, A28). Graduate assistant unions or organizing campaigns are now active at more than thirty universities (Lachelier 2002, 31). The University of Wisconsin recognized a graduate student union as far back as 1969 (2002, 31). In the private arena, Yale graduate assistants began campaigning for recognition in 1987 and successfully engineered their now famous strike in 1995 (*YaleUnions* n.d.). Most recently, the proposed graduate assistants union at the University of Illinois won its election by a 3 to 1 majority to become a bargaining unit of over 2,000 employees (Forrest 2002, 1).

The unionization wave began at public universities, where graduate assistants were state employees subject to state rather than federal labor laws (Joseph and Curtiss 1997, B6). Private universities came under the jurisdiction of the National Labor Relations Board ("NLRB"), which had previously held that the status of student-employees was determined by a "primary purpose" test that in effect excluded graduate assistants as employees from coverage under the National Labor Relations Act (Rowland 2001, 941). This changed in April 2000 when the NLRB discarded its long-standing test, applied a new "compensation services" test to determine the status of graduate assistants, and granted recognition and the right to organize to graduate assistants at New York University (*N.Y. University*, 2000 NLRB LEXIS 7480). The decision was appealed to federal district court; despite amicus briefs filed by seven major universities and several higher education councils, the Board's decision has so far been upheld (Lafer 2001, 63). Graduate student and adjunct faculty unionization can be viewed as a logical response to the recent shift in university management to the business model. As universities operate more and more like businesses, the lowest paid and most disenfranchised workers have responded as they might in large manufacturing facilities, by unionizing in the hopes of securing better working conditions (Lydersen 2000, 5).

Libraries are even closer to a business model in operation, and their workers have historically been low paid (Berry 1991, 6). New alliances between various collective bargaining units on individual campuses have been forged within the time frame of the growth of the Living Wage campaign (HERE News 2002). These alliances are likely to continue based on the results achieved by consolidated action on behalf of Living Wage campaigns (Woomer 2001). The attention and pressure on academic libraries to offer better wages and working conditions will only intensify with this consolidated action.

Origins of the Student–Labor Alliance

The origins of the alliance between undergraduate students and organized labor should be briefly examined to appreciate its possible continuing impact on university and academic library labor matters.

In 1996, the AFL-CIO under John Sweeney instituted a four-week intern program for college students called Union Summer. (In fact, the Union Summer program was part of Sweeney's campaign platform in his quest for the AFL-CIO presidency in 1995.) (Greenhouse 1996, A18). Over the course of five years, some 2,300 interns received basic training in union organizing (AFL-CIO n.d-a.). The interns were largely college students; they received a few days' training in labor history and organizing techniques and then were sent out "in the field," where they participated in various labor/organizing campaigns around the country. In some instances, the unionizing efforts supported by the students were among workers on university campuses.

The AFL-CIO's Web page on Union Summer listed the following Union Summer experience in Cleveland:

> Hotel Employees & Restaurant Employees Local 10 put 10 Summeristas to work on a variety of campaigns in which the union is involved. Their major project was research on Case Western Reserve University, where the local hopes to launch a campaign to represent cafeteria workers in the near future. Along with the research, the USAs signed workers on to the living wage campaign, probing and gathering information the local will also use in its organizing drive. (AFL-CIO n.d.-a)

This program has been a significant impetus for galvanizing what have been randomly expressed concerns on globalization, corporatization of universities, and low wages into organized student campaigns and movements (Lachelier 2002, 31). The Union Summer Web page also notes that as a 1997 Summerista:

> Laura McSpedon became intrigued by what she learned about the power of regular folks in changing conditions around them. So upon return to school at Georgetown University in Washington, D.C., Laura became active with her school's anti-sweatshops campaign. (AFL-CIO n.d.-b)

Most important, this kind of involvement in the anti-sweatshop movement on campuses spread quite easily into other campus labor issues, beginning with involvement in local Living Wage campaigns:

> "While we were doing our anti-sweat work, we talked to a lot of people who said, You've got to look at what is going on here. . . . With the energy and momentum from winning (the anti-sweatshop) campaign, we felt we had the strength to move on" Becky Moran quoted in *The Nation*. (Manners 2001, 6)

One of the original Summeristas, Dan Hennefeld, helped start the Progressive Student Labor Movement upon his return to Harvard. That organization led the 2001 sit-in at Harvard; three other organizers of the sit-in were also Union Summer participants. Union Summer grads have also been active in the labor movements and sweatshop campaigns at Duke, Brown, Georgetown, and state universities such as Connecticut, Tennessee, and Wisconsin (Manners 2001).

At Harvard, the involvement spilled over to the collective bargaining process between the university and the SEIU. Another Harvard sit-in participant was quoted in the *Nation* as saying: "The unions are very receptive to this idea of working together. . . . If the unions and students work together, that's pretty serious"(Manners 2001, 17).

Lasting Effects

It was pretty amazing. There was almost a kind of social fission as class and race lines were crossed. We had spoken with workers for a long time leading up to this, so it wasn't like we didn't know each other before, but being in the struggle together brought us to a new level. Not since the 1930's has there been an alliance like the one we're seeing now between students and workers, as far as I know.—Harvard sit-in organizer, Maple Rasza quoted in Salon.com. (Colin 2002)

Will an alliance that is more akin to an emotional tie between a romanticized concept of "workers " and students while school is in session fade away like the latest fad, or will a true alliance between students and organized labor, as envisioned by Sweeney in 1995, continue to flourish and effect change?

An October 2002 issue of the *Kiplinger Newsletter* predicted a renewed wave of labor media drives in 2003, which would provide more opportunities for partnering (Scott 2002). Unions like Hotel Employees and Restaurant Employees (HERE) are by now invested in and dependent upon student support for their organizing activity. HERE counts a successfully negotiated first contract for food service workers at SUNY Binghamton as a recent example of the strength of the alliance with students. (HERE News 2002).

The SEIU organized a tour of Harvard janitors and students to campuses across the country to garner support for their cause. Once again, the leap from the lowest paid group of campus employees to library workers is not far.

As for the continued commitment of students to the alliance with labor, the Student Labor Action Project (SLAP) has expanded its planning and implementation of a National Student Labor Day of Action begun in 2000 to a National Student Labor Week of Action in 2003 (Student Labor Action Project 2003).

The alliance was alive and well this past fall when UCLA agreed to voluntary union recognition for 140 campus dining workers by its AFSCME local, several weeks after students and workers packed a board meeting of the food service contracting firm and presented a petition supporting the workers signed by 1,400 students (Salonga 2002).

The opening of a published letter from the as yet unrecognized graduate student union coordinating committee to Yale president Levin gives every indication of well-cemented relations between labor and students:

30 September 2002
Dear President Levin,

On Wednesday, September 25, nearly 200 graduate and professional students were arrested *along with our partners in the Federation of Hospital and University Employees* (emphasis added). (*YaleUnions* n.d.)

Another, more subtle indication of the staying power of the new labor movement, which has forged an alliance not only with students but with the university as well, is the emergence and continued growth and development of the labor-backed Institute for Labor and Employment ("ILE") , created at the University of California in 2000. In the years following World War II, industrial relations institutes proliferated at universities like Cornell, Columbia, Wisconsin, Michigan State, Princeton, Illinois, Berkeley, and UCLA. Programs like these have not been created for some time.

The mission of this new institute, the ILE, is boldly stated:

> The ILE was founded on July 1, 2000 by an act of the California state legislature, recognizing the vital importance of new research about labor and workplace issues and the preeminent role of labor in California as a trendsetter for the nation. (www.ucla.edu/ile)

The ILE is openly pro-labor, and its mission is to build a bridge between universities and labor. Research projects funded through the ILE will be of enormous benefit to the labor movement at large. Graduate students at the ILE will likely include many of those former Union Summer interns and campus anti-sweatshop campaign organizers. For example, the ILE at UC Riverside hosted a conference in 2002 on Living Wage campaigns and their social impact (UCLA 2002).

In short, if the ILE is indeed a bellwether and California is indeed a national trendsetter, ILE, the Living Wage campaign, and the anti-sweatshop movements are producing the new generation of intellectuals and leaders, committed to reestablishing the preeminence of labor in the workplace. In their eyes the workplace includes the university, and the students are its natural agents.

Future Student Activity in University Labor Matters

Students have focused on global labor issues, on local or campus labor issues, and on themselves as labor issues.

Recent events at the University of Massachusetts, where the United Auto Workers won a campaign to represent resident assistants of the university's dormitories, are indicative of the potential growth of this movement (Hoover 2002, A38). Resident assistants are undergraduates. The possibility of widespread unions for undergraduate students carries enormous significance for any campus unit that employs students. This is of particular concern for libraries, which typically employ large numbers of student workers.

The NLRB limited recognition of graduate students as employees to teaching assistants; however, the University of Massachusetts case suggests potential (at least in state universities) for including other types of graduate students (such as research assistants, including library science students) and undergraduates (resident assistants) as employees (Brill 2002).

Unionization in Academic Libraries

In addition to graduate student unionization trends, there has been recent research concerning the effect of unionization among academic librarians

A study conducted by Garcha and Phillips of the University of Toledo examined participation by academic librarians in local and national faculty unions and concluded that not only did they earn higher salaries, but librarians also viewed unionization as a vehicle for greater involvement in decision-making processes (2001, 126–27). In contrast to that study, the twenty-year history of collective bargaining by librarians at Wayne State University shows lost ground in recent years on tenure and promotion rights as well as sabbatical options (Spang 1993, 251).

A study published by Tina Hovekamp in 1995 concluded that the presence of unions among librarians in academic institutions bore a negative relationship to job satisfaction. However, that relationship was not determined to be a product of union culture. Salary was shown to be the most accurate predictor of job satisfaction (Hovekamp 1995, 349). Yet Hovekamp's study also showed that union presence was a negative predictor of organizational loyalty (1995, 305).

As with graduate students, the motivation for unionization among librarians is to gain greater self-determination. Participative management practices by administrators will go far in improving perceptions of the work environment.

Measures for Library Administrators

With continued student interest in university labor issues and the promise of continued consolidated efforts by separate collective bargaining units and other interest groups both likely, what measures can library administrators take to guarantee not only good labor relations but, more important, a workforce interested in the work of the library rather than in working with students? Given the prospect of advancing library technology resulting in obsolete jobs and smaller workforce needs, what can administrators do to assuage staff anxieties and redirect their interests from defensive measures like alliances with students and other collective bargaining units?

Support staff jobs must be rejuvenated, and prospects for growth must be promoted to discourage and prevent staff alienation. Employees must be able to first look within the library for the means for upward mobility. Library administrators must take the risk and the initiative to institute creative ways of doing library work that provide career growth opportunities for employees. To supplement more traditional human resources approaches such as salary surveys conducted to measure comparable market compensation trends, suggested strategies include the following:

1. Constant attention and development of a staff communications process, designed to promote staff awareness rather than whispers along the grapevine.

2. Development and implementation of formal and meaningful career development programs that focus on and award competencies, thus taking the emphasis away from available positions and placing it on the employee.

3. Ongoing analysis of staff demographics to ensure that the workplace is providing appropriate operational and structural support for staff individual and family needs.

4. Ongoing review of the physical environment and workspace to ensure that it is supportive of and appropriate to the work being done.

5. Continued and visible efforts to partner with unions (where applicable) on quality of work life programs.

Renewed emphasis on quality of work life and participative management are the only real preventative measures, not only to union organizing, but also to adversarial labor relations.

References

ACORN. n.d. *Living Wage for Colleges & Universities.* Available: http://www.acorn.org/acorn10/livingwage/campus/index.html. (Accessed January 10, 2003).

AFL-CIO. n.d-a. *Union Summer Questions and Answers.* Available: http:www.aflcio.org/aboutunion/unionsummer/qopage.cfm. (Accessed January 10, 2003).

AFL-CIO. n.d-b. *What's Become of Our Summeristas.* Available: http:www.aflcio.org/unionsummer/summeristas. (Accessed December 19, 2002).

Bernstein, Aaron. 1999. "Sweatshop Reform: How to Solve the Standoff." *Business Week* 3 (May): 86

Berry, J. 1991. "Why Don't They Run It Like a Business?" *Library Journal* (May 15): 6.

Brill, Edward. 2002. "Private universities appeal NLRB decisions on graduate student union." *HR on Campus* (July 2).

Colin, Chris. 2002. "Welcome to the Occupation." *Salon.com,* (June 6) Available: http://archive.salon.com/mwt/feature/2002/06/03/rasza. (Accessed January 3, 2003).

Forrest, Sharrita. 2002. "Graduate Students OK Unionization." *Inside Illinois* (December 6): 1.

Garcha, R., and J. Phillips. 2001. "U.S. Academic Librarians: Their Involvement in Union Activities." *Library Review* 50, no. 3:126–127.

Greenhouse, Steven. 1996. "Labor Leader Plans Little Steps to Big Economic Goal." *New York Times* (February 16) A-18.

Hoover, Eric. 2002. "Unionized Resident Assistants and UMass Will Begin Collective Bargaining." *Chronicle of Higher Education* (August 16). A38.

Hotel Employees Restaurant Employees (HERE) News. 2002. *Binghamton Food Service Workers Win First Service Contract.* (November 20). Available: http:hereunion.org/herenews/021120binghamton.html. (Accessed January 2, 2003).

Hovekamp, Tina. 1994. "Organizational Commitment of Professional Employees in Union and Nonunion Research Libraries." *College & Research Libraries* (July):: 305.

Hovekamp, Tina. 1995. "Unionization and Job Satisfaction among Professional Library Employees in Academic Research Institutions." *College & Research Libraries* (July): 349.

Johnson, Paul. 2000. "Resurgence of Labor As A Citizenship Movement In The New Labor Relations Environment." *Critical Sociology* (July): 139–40.

Joseph, T., and J. Curtiss. 1997. "Why Professors Should Support Graduate-Student Unions." *Chronicle of Higher Education* (February 21): B6.

Krueger, Alan. 2001. "At Colleges, Prosperity Lifts Expectations." *New York Times* (April 26). Available: http://www.nytimes.com/2001/04/26/business/26SCEN.html. (Accessed January 10, 2003).

Lachelier, Paul. 2002. "Making History, Making Democracy Un-Extraordinary: Harvard Students Make History." *Radical Teacher* (March 31): 31.

Lafer, Gordon. 2001. "Graduate Students Fight the Corporate University." *Dissent* (Fall): 63.

Leatherman, Courtney. 1998. "Part-time Instructors Vote to Unionize at Chicago's Columbia College." *Chronicle of Higher Education* (February 13): A16.

Lewis, Diane. 1996. "Labor '96: Unions Look to the Young." *Boston Globe* (September 2): A1.

Lexis-Nexis. (Accessed via Princeton University Library server). Available: http://web.lexis-nexis.com/universe/docuaid-md5=41130911137a4deec 966f935d97a12c4. (Accessed January 10, 2003).

Lydersen, Kari. 2000. "Mad Grads." *In These Times* (May 29): 5.

Manners, Jane. 2001. "Joe Hill Goes to Harvard." *The Nation* (July 2). Available: www.thenation.com/doc.mhtml?20010702&cs=manners. (Accessed January 10, 2003).

Milgram, Jeff. 2001. "Nassau Hall Target of Worker Rally." *Princeton Packet* (April 10). Available: www.zwire.com/site/n...023& BRD=1870&PAG=461&dept_id. (Accessed January 10, 2003).

Moberg, David. 2002. "Too Cruel for School." *In These Times* (May 27): 21.

Robinson, Ian. 2000. "Neoliberal Restructuring and U.S. Union: Toward Social Movement Unionism." *Critical Sociology* 26, nos. 1–2 (July): 8.

Rowland, Joshua. "Forecasts of Doom: The Dubious Threat of Graduate Teaching Assistant Collective Bargaining to Academic Freedom" Boston *College Law Review* July, 2001: 941–943.

Salonga, R. "ASUCLA workers get fulltime status". *Daily Bruin,* 30 September 2002. 10 January 2003 http://www.dailybruin.ucla.edu/ news/home.asp.

Schneider, Alison. "Adjuncts at Roosevelt U. Vote to Unionize" *Chronicle of Higher Education* 13 February 1998: A28.

Scott, Dean. 2002. "Labor Unions Push for Service-Sector Gains." *Kiplinger Business Forecasts* (October 31). Available: http://web. lexis-nexis.com/universe/docuaid-md5=41130911137a4deec966f9 35d97a12c4. (Accessed December 17, 2002).

Spang, Lothar. 1993. "Collective Bargaining and Faculty Status: A Twenty-Year Case Study of Wayne State University Librarians." *College & Research Libraries* (May): 251.

Student Labor Action Project. 2003. "2003 National Student Labor Week of Action: March 31–April 4." Available: http://www.jwj.org/SLAP/ A4/2003.htm. (Accessed October 26, 2003).

Tilly, Chris. 2001. "Next Steps: For the Living-Wage Movement." *Dollars&Sense* 237. (September–October). Available: http://www. dollarsandsense.org/archives/2001/0901tilly. (Accessed October 26, 2003).

UCLA. 2002. A Conference on the Living Wage Movement: Building a Research Agenda, February 22, University of California Riverside. Available: http://www.ucop.edu/ile/conferences/living_wage/index.html. (Accessed October 26, 2003).

Wallack, Juliette. 2002. "Library Staff Set to Stage Friday Walkout." *Brown Daily Herald* (October 23). Available: http://browndailyherald.com/stories.cfm?S=O&ID=7615. (Accessed January 10, 2003).

Woomer, Nicholas. 2001. "The Student Labor Union." *Alternative Press.* (Accessed via Princeton University Library server). (Accessed November 25, 2002).

YaleUnions. n.d. Available: http://www.yaleunions.org/geso/index.htm. (Accessed January 10, 2003).

Zahra, Tara. 1999. "Sweating the Big Stuff." *Salon.com* (August 6) Available: http://www.salon.com/books/it/1999/08/06/sweatshop/index.html. (Accessed December 1, 2002).

9

Compensation Management in the Academic Library

Teri R. Switzer

The role of the human resource specialist in the academic library is evolving from that of a processor of salary and benefit packages to a strategic partner in determining total compensation. This more proactive role in the process of setting salary and benefits standards is a critical component in the recruitment and retention of librarians and library support staff. However, to be effective, it is important that human resource specialists have a thorough understanding of all facets of total compensation.

Total compensation consists of two elements, salary and benefits, both of which have a monetary as well as a nonmonetary component. This chapter offers a broad overview of both salary (also referred to as compensation) and benefits and the roles the parent institution and the library play in determining total compensation.

Compensation Overview

One's salary is a critical component of the employment relationship. The concept of receiving remuneration for work performed has been around since the beginning of time. However, in today's world the concept of trading and working for goods and food has nearly been lost. In the early twentieth century, the federal government took a significant role and began to introduce several changes in many aspects of how workers were paid. One of the more significant acts, the Fair Labor Standards Act of 1938, dictated equal pay for equal work.

Although recessions dotted the following twenty years, the economy boomed, and the federal government played an increasingly important role in the American workplace. The Bureau of Labor Statistics conducted wage surveys, and the Equal Pay Act, Executive Order 11246, Title 7 of the Civil Rights Act, was ratified in 1963. This act is probably one of the most important pieces of legislation to provide additional stabilization of wages.

Compensation in the 1970s was affected by recession, inflation, and high unemployment, but the trend to improve and equalize wages continued. In 1974 the Social Security Act was amended to provide for automatic cost-of-living adjustments and, shortly after, the Employment Cost Index (ECI) began to pave the way for a more standardized measure of salaries and benefits.

The next two decades were marked by prosperity. The majority of the legislation enacted dealt with benefits, but in 1990 Congress passed the Federal Employees Pay Comparability Act (FEPCA), which created a process of combining national and local pay adjustments. Soon all the existing occupational area and industry wage surveys were combined into one single survey that would collect locality pay data, the Occupational Compensation Survey, on which many library support staff (civil service) positions are based (Schwenk and Pfuntner 2001). This worked well for several years but, wanting a more umbrella approach to the collection and processing of compensation data, the Bureau of Labor Statistics decided to create the National Compensation Survey in 1997. The National Compensation Survey is proving to be a flexible, comprehensive attempt to provide wage and benefits data (Schwenk and Pfuntner 2001).

Compensation Trends

Workers in the twenty-first century will undoubtedly continue to reap some of the benefits of such acts as the Vocational Education Act of 1963 and the Concentrated Employment and Training Act of 1973, which provided for collecting d unemployment and poverty information detailed by geographic area. In addition, the establishment of the Cost of Living Council to provide guidelines on wage and price escalation has led to additional emphasis on wage statistics and on what today's workers get paid relative to the prices of goods.

Regardless of the effects legislation has had on salaries in general, compensation continues to be influenced by several factors that are producing some important trends in compensating workers. One of these trends is aligning wages to the organization's goals. As local, state, and federal budgets become limited due to a poor economy, many libraries find themselves being stretched thin and are having to find ways to more efficiently use their employees. Employee compensation that is tied to productivity and performance as it relates to the organization's output is normally known as variable pay and is a form of pay-for-performance. Examples of pay-for-performance are merit increases based on performance ratings and monetary stipends given for successful grant writing. As performance becomes more tied to skills and knowledge, some libraries are finding themselves rewarding employees not only for being productive and good performers but also for acquiring additional skills and knowledge critical to the continued success of the organization.

Another trend is tailoring compensation to the needs of employees (Schwenk and Pfuntner 2001). This can take on many different forms, from health insurance plans to campus child care to choices between defined benefit and defined contribution retirement plans. The main focus is the flexibility to better meet the employee's personal and professional needs. Even though these forms of compensation generally fall under the auspices of the parent institution, the library can still offer additional incentives such as flexible work arrangements and job sharing.

A third trend in compensation is not a new concept but has become one of the primary focuses of the American Library Association: better salaries and pay equity. During the twentieth century there was improvement in all aspects of compensation. The per capita income in 1900 was $4,200 in 1999 dollars, compared to $33,700 in 1999 (Fisk 2001). The number of people employed during the twentieth century increased 600 percent. In addition, whereas only 19 percent of age-eligible women were working in 1900, 60 percent of age-eligible women in 1999 were employed. However, the quest for fair and equitable wages for all workers is not yet finished. There are still millions of working people living in poverty. The crux of the matter is that working forty hours a week at minimum wage provides an income more than $7,000 lower than the 2002 poverty line for the typical family of four (Center for Policy Alternatives 2002). Fortunately, many cities, including Baltimore, Boston, Chicago, Cleveland, Des Moines, Detroit, Los Angeles, Milwaukee, Minneapolis, New York City, San Antonio, San Francisco, and St. Louis, have adopted what is called a "living wage." The "living wage" proposes a rate of $8.50 per hour, which provides an income that is just below the current federal poverty level for a family of four.

Although this is a start in the campaign for lower income workers to earn better salaries, there is still a long way to go. One of the issues that still must be addressed is the discrepancy between salaries paid to men and those paid to women. According to the National Committee on Pay Equity (2001), this wage gap has narrowed from 62 percent in 1982 to 73 percent in 2000. This is promising, but it is primarily due to the fall in men's earnings rather than an increase in women's salaries.

The Women's Equal Pay Act of 1945 was the first bill introduced in Congress that addressed pay equity, but equal pay for equal work was not mandated until eighteen years later. Even though the Pay Equity Act prohibits unfairly compensating individuals for equal work, and Title VII of the Civil Rights Act broadened the Pay Equity Act to include race, color, sex, and religious or national origin as factors prohibited in wage discrimination, there are still concerns about professions that have been undervalued, which are typically performed by women and therefore are low paying.

The Bureau of Labor Statistics reports that the outlook for library employment is better than average at least until 2006. Technical expertise and skills will be sought and will aid in warranting higher salaries. In 2001, the average salary for new library and information services graduates was $36,818, which is much greater than the inflation rate of 1.3 percent, and 5.49 percent greater than the previous year (Terrell 2002). The 2002 Special Library Association salary survey reported that the median salary for full-time information professionals in Canada as of April 1, 2002, was $56,653, and the median salary for U.S. information professionals was $56,500. The average salaries were $59,328 and $60,583 respectively. These salaries are an increase from the prior year of 2.4 percent for Canadian information professionals and 3.7 percent for those in the United States.

If we turn our attention solely to academic libraries, there are other variables that the human resource specialist should consider when addressing salary issues. One of these is that salaries in private academic libraries exceeded those in publicly supported academic libraries by 6.4 percent during fiscal year 2002 (Kyrillidou and Young 2002). A second variable is the number of librarians in a given institution. Those libraries with a greater number of librarians typically pay higher salaries for nearly all positions. Specifically, libraries with MLS staff of 75 to 110 had the highest average salary, whereas libraries with 22 to 49 MLS staff were the lowest (Kyrillidou and Young 2002).

Geographic region is another factor in the salary equation, with the highest salaries being paid in the Pacific West, New England, and Middle Atlantic states respectively. The lowest salaries in U.S. libraries are in the East South Central region. And, as a result of a ten-year decline in purchasing power, Canada has the lowest average salary.

The salaries for library assistants tend to be lower still. In a five-state region consisting of Colorado, Wyoming, Kansas, New Mexico, and Utah, the mean hourly wage for library assistants was a little more than $8.00 per hour (*Fast Facts* 2000). This wage just passes the poverty line for a family of three ($15,000) and falls short of that for a family of four ($18,100).

Although the salary increases mentioned above rival those realized in 1998 and 1999, the average salary in the profession does not come close to salaries in other comparable professions with comparable educational requirements. And therein lies one of the obstacles that human resource specialists have to confront when recruiting and retaining information specialists. Salaries in library-related positions are known to be low. And although these wages have improved, they are still among the lowest. Salary data collected by the Association of College and Research Libraries reflect an upward trend in college and university librarian salaries. Nonetheless, when compared to academic teaching faculty salaries, academic librarian salaries are an average of at least 10 percent lower (Terrell and Gregory 2003).

Various strategies can be employed when addressing salary inequities. Some institutions are beginning to look at broad banding as a tool to more equitably structure pay scales using a broader range of duties and responsibilities. Other libraries structure their salaries for librarians and support staff who do not fall under a state or federal wage scale by using the variable or at-risk pay concept. Still others use a hybrid approach that combines a cost-of-living index factor with a performance factor. Finally, some libraries use a competency model in which the changing roles of librarians and support staff are reflected in the skills and knowledge needed for the positions. These skills are then written into the job descriptions and, in turn, become part of the evaluation process.

Strategies for Higher Salaries

Although the human resource specialist has some control over the salaries in his or her individual library, the issue is more widespread and needs to be addressed on a broader scale. The Better Salaries/Pay Equity Task Force, created by Mitch Freedman, 2003 American Library Association president, focuses on pay equity issues in the library profession. The task force's mission is to "provide librarians and library workers with the information, resources and tools to enable them to advocate and negotiate, individually or collectively, for improved compensation and pay equity" (*Better Salaries/Pay Equity Task Force Mission* 2002).

Among the strategies that the task force has outlined are two that academic library human resource specialists should consider to become more active advocates for better salaries for present and potential employees. The first is the strategic use of communication to build a more thorough understanding of and support for better salaries. In times of fiscal challenges, university and library administration tend to use the declining economy as an excuse for lower raises and not increasing the starting base salary. It is the human resource specialist's responsibility to convince administratorsto commit to rectifying the salary inequities that exist and to assist in developing a plan and a timetable for addressing them. Various approaches can be considered, including the following:

- Collect information on salary ranges of comparable professions (include those in which a master's degree is a minimum qualification).

- Obtain information on campus faculty salary ranges (including averages for each professorial rank) from the campus's institutional research office.

- Compare library salaries with both those of comparable professions and academic faculty.

Once these data are laid out and the discrepancies are noted, a plan for addressing the inequities should be constructed. Depending on the dollar amount needed to put all outlying salaries into line, a phase-in approach may be needed.

This could be handled in a number of ways. Longevity, rank, average of overall performance evaluations, and level of responsibilities are measures that could be used to determine which salary group should be addressed first. Another avenue might be to concentrate on those with the largest dollar amount discrepancy first. Once a plan is put into place, library administrators should consider requesting financial assistance from the university's administration. If this avenue is used, be prepared to show the rationale and the plan, as well as the financial contribution the library will make.

Another approach uses internal salary comparisons and is more effective when addressing salary compression. There have been different versions of this approach, but the one implemented at the University of Colorado at Boulder Norlin Library has become a model for addressing salary inequities. This approach uses a statistical study in which a professional experience score is used to identify inequities among the librarians. Longevity, prior experience, and research experience are all weighted to give a score. A multiple regression analysis is then used to identify those librarians whose actual salaries do not coincide with projected salaries (Seaman 1999).

Regardless of the approach taken, it is important to clearly identify and describe the added value a library's employees bring to the campus, the university, and the community. Every library employee should prepare an annual self-report detailing accomplishments and successes. If these reports are to be seen outside the library, wording should be used that makes sense to non-library personnel. Furthermore, if negotiations or discussions take place with university administrators, it is advisable to educate them on the complexities of academic library positions and how these duties and responsibilities relate to what they, the administrators, do.

The second strategy identified by the Better Salaries/Pay Equity Task Force involves building partnerships and finding allies. Working with unions can be an effective strategy in advocating for better salaries (2002). Union librarians make an average of 37 percent more than those not associated with a union, and union support staff make approximately 42 percent more than non-union staff (*Union Membership and Earnings Data Book* 2001). Collective bargaining plays a critical role in the salary negotiation process. Unions have been involved in salary disputes for many years, and by using their political clout they can advocate quite successfully for both librarian and support staff salaries. However, only 17 to 21 percent of library workers are unionized (*Union Membership and Earnings Data Book* 2001). Yet there are still allies the human resource specialist can connect with to become a more ardent advocate for better salaries:

- Subscribe to *Moneytalks* (www.mjfreedman.org/moneytalks.html), an informative, active discussion list where library workers can share strategies and information on how to improve library salaries.

- Check out the AFL-CIO (www.aflcio.org/home.htm) to become familiar with union contracts and learn guidelines on salary negotiating.

- Become more familiar with your university's and your state's salary guidelines and salary ranges. Become involved in your state's personnel board and work toward revising job descriptions for librarians and support staff.

- Work with your state library association to sponsor information sessions and workshops on how to better advocate for better salaries. Help form a committee to address salary issues.

Benefits Overview

Although monetary compensation is an essential component in the recruitment and retention process, benefits are equally important and can often be the deciding factor in whether a candidate accepts an offer or a present employee stays. As the competition increases for library employees with the skills and knowledge that most academic libraries need, many libraries rely on their benefit packages to give them the leading edge. It is important for today's human resource specialists to be informed about the various benefits available so that they can judicially converse with recruits and employees.

Fringe benefits first came on the employment scene in 1943 when the War Labor Board offered medical insurance and retirement plans. These benefits were exempt from the Wage Stabilization Act and provided a type of counterbalance to the frozen pay levels that were implemented to control inflation. Since that time, benefit packages have played an increasingly important role in the recruitment and retention of employees. According to the United States Chamber of Commerce (2003), employee benefits accounted for 39 percent of payroll costs in 2001. Medical benefits accounted for approximately 11 percent, time compensation for 10 percent, and retirement plans for 8 percent. There are two categories of benefits offered to library employees: those provided by the parent institution and those offered by the library.

University-Supported Benefits

Academic institutions typically offer a wide range of benefits to their employees. As university employees, academic librarians are afforded the same institutional benefits as all other university employees. There are several kinds of benefits offered by a library's parent institution, including retirement plans; medical, dental, and vision insurance; sick and annual leave; educational leave; and sabbatical leave.

Retirement Plans

Pensions were introduced in the early 1900s but weren't regulated until the economic disaster of the 1930s, which paved the way for the Social Security Act. The Social Security Act has played a vital role in shaping the retirement system that we have today because it provided a federal system of old-age benefits for retired workers and a federal-state system of unemployment insurance. In 1965 the Social Security Act was amended to include Medicare.

The next piece of significant legislation affecting retirement security was passed in 1974. The Employee Retirement Income Security Act (ERISA) regulated private pensions and imposed financial and accounting controls. ERISA provided a sense of security for workers; in the event that a pension plan was terminated, the workers who had contributed to that plan would be entitled to their vested pension benefits. In 1978 the Revenue Act was ratified, which allowed for the creation of 401(k) defined contribution retirement plans as well as pretax contributions to many different savings vehicles.

Defined Contribution Plans

The retirement plans most commonly offered in academic libraries are defined contribution plans and defined benefit plans. Defined contribution plans oblige employees to contribute a certain amount of their salaries to an approved plan each year. The payouts are based on profits and tend to be riskier than defined benefit plans. Examples of defined contribution plans are 401(k) plans, Individual Retirement Accounts (IRAs), stock option plans, and profit-sharing plans. Generally academic libraries offer what are called money purchase pension plans and savings and thrift plans. Money purchase plans are those in which an employer contributes a fixed amount, generally calculated as a percentage of the employee's salary. Some plans allow the employee to also make a contribution, but most do not. The savings and thrift plans call for employee contributions, which are then matched in some percent by the employer.

There are several attractive features to defined contribution plans, including early withdrawal for personal as well as hardship cases, although most early withdrawals incur tax penalties; the capability to borrow against the account; the right to roll over the account; and the ability to receive a lump sum payment or an annuity upon retirement. The right of the employee to the retirement benefit generally is allowed immediately upon enrolling in the plan. However, some plans do not allow for immediate full vesting. Instead, they may offer graduated vesting, in which the percentage of employer contributions that is not forfeited increases over time, and cliff vesting, in which there is a specific time over which the accounts are deemed vested. Of the defined contribution retirement plans available to academic libraries, the savings and thrift plans are more commonly offered.

Defined Benefit Plans

Defined benefit plans put the risk on the employer; they guarantee a set payout amount once the employee retires. As with defined contribution plans, there are several appealing components to defined benefit plans. Retirement benefits can be paid out by one of four methods: lump sum payment; straight life annuity, in which a periodic payment is made for the life of the retiree but survivors do not receive additional payments; joint and survivor annuity as detailed in ERISA; and percent of unreduced accrued benefit, in which a retiree's spouse will receive a proportional amount upon the death of the retiree. Defined benefit plans offer nearly the same vesting privileges as the defined contribution plans, with the exception that any Social Security benefits afforded the retiree offset the defined benefit payment. A second difference between the two plans is that defined benefit plans allow for pension increases that are adjusted to the Consumer Price Index. A third major difference between the two plans is that defined benefit plans generally cannot be 100 percent transferred or rolled over to another retirement vehicle. However, the retiree's personal contribution can be withdrawn and reinvested as desired. For employees who may want to move to a different state, the portability component is important. Many state/publicly supported institutions have a state retirement plan that is regarded as a defined benefit plan.

Some academic institutions offer a type of hybrid of a defined contribution plan plus mandatory contribution into Medicare or Social Security. Depending on the defined benefit plan, contribution into Medicare or Social Security may or may not be offered. Employees who may have worked under a Social Security plan in a previous job and have earned forty quarters of service will be able to collect Social Security upon retirement and will be covered by Medicare. The issue that often hits employees who do not pay into Social Security is that they may not be covered by Medicare upon retirement. Therefore, those institutions that offer or mandate contribution into Medicare or Social Security in addition to a defined contribution plan or a defined benefit plan quite often have more appeal to some employees.

Medical Insurance Coverage

One of the more contentious and sought after benefits is medical insurance. During the past twenty years, the health care industry has experienced an unprecedented rise in health care expenditures and, therefore, an increase in employer health care costs. In 2001, health care costs accounted for 5.6 percent of compensation costs (Baker and Diaz 2001). Each year health care insurance costs increase, which is having a profound effect on the kind and level of medical insurance offered by many academic institutions. Most academic institutions cover a substantial portion of employees' health care premiums, but with those premiums increasing, institutions are beginning to re-evaluate the kind and level of plans offered.

There are various medical insurance plans, but the more common ones are traditional fee-for-service, preferred provider plans (PPOs), in which participants choose from a network of medical providers, and any care received from an out of network provider is only partially reimbursed; exclusive provider organization plans (EPOs), in which participants use medical providers from the specified network and there is no coverage for care received from an out of network provider; and health maintenance organizations (HMOs), in which care is given the participant for a fixed, prepaid fee by a variety of medical personnel.

The specific components of each health care plan tend to be complicated, but frequently the additional items covered by the health care plan are what are desirable. These include coverage for mental health and substance abuse treatment centers, prescription drugs, vision care, dental care, and alternative medical care (including nutritional supplements/herbal treatment, massage, acupuncture, and chiropractic).

Although federal law does not require a university to offer Consolidated Omnibus Budget Reconciliation Act (COBRA) health care continuation coverage to former employees, many universities make COBRA an option upon resignation or retirement. COBRA gives former employees the right to temporary continuation of health insurance coverage at group rates.

Other Insurance

Workers' compensation insurance is an important but often disregarded component in the benefit package. Even though being a library worker might seem to be one of the safest professions as far as work injury is concerned, it is actually among those with high work-related injuries. Carpel tunnel syndrome and other repetitive stress/motion injuries have become increasingly common in libraries due to the repetitive nature of work such as using computers, handling books, and scanning bar codes. State workers' compensation laws realized vast changes in 2002. Alaska, California, Colorado, Florida, Georgia, Idaho, Kansas, Kentucky, Maine, Maryland, Minnesota, New Jersey, New York, Oklahoma, Pennsylvania, Rhode Island, South Dakota, Tennessee, Vermont, Virginia, and Wyoming all addressed some part of their workers' compensation laws, with changes ranging from revising the eligibility for disability benefits, to increasing the maximum benefit for temporary and permanent total disability, to increasing the amount of death benefit (Whittington 2003). In most cases, workers' compensation insurance covers employees both at work and outside of work, but not on work-related business such as attending conferences, off-campus workshops, and meetings.

Short-term and long-term disability benefits are also significant components when considering benefits. Typically, short-term disability benefits provide for a salary replacement of anywhere from 50 to 60 percent of the base salary for a specified period of time, usually less than a year. Some academic institutions routinely cover civil service or similar employees while offering optional short-term disability insurance for a small fee to administrative staff and faculty. Long-term disability insurance provides similar coverage but generally has no time limitation and can continue until retirement age is reached.

Many people routinely subscribe to life insurance; however, many others do not. It is not uncommon for academic institutions to require their administrative employees and faculty to hold a minimum amount of life insurance coverage. Some institutions will provide minimal life insurance coverage for their faculty and administrators as part of the benefit package. Others will offer a variety of life insurance (term and whole life) at reduced group rates.

One of the more obscure, yet important, insurance policies normally offered by academic institutions is liability insurance. Many states have a state governmental immunity act that protects public employees from liability and from the cost of defense when the claim against the public employee arises out of injuries sustained from an act or omission of that employee occurring during the performance of duties and within the scope of that person's employment.

Leave Benefits

Several types of leave are offered by academic institutions, including personal sick, family sick, annual/vacation, administrative, military, funeral, and jury. Paid leaves such as these significantly expand the benefits package and can provide not only indirect compensation but also the flexibility to better meet the employee's personal and professional needs. The amount of leave can vary from one to two or more days per month, and will depend on what the leave is. Jury duty and funeral leave are more common among state-supported institutions and those with union employees (Simpson 1997).

Among legislation that affects leave, the Family Medical Leave Act (FMLA) has had the most impact on and benefit to workers. FMLA was enacted in 1993 and requires employers to grant employees up to twelve weeks of time off (either with pay when using sick or vacation leave or without pay) for personal serious illness, to care for an ill dependent or parent, or for the birth or adoption of a child.

Other Benefits

Many academic institutions also offer access to flexible spending accounts and credit unions; promotion stipends; benefits replacement pay, which can take the form of money included in one's monthly salary to be applied toward such items as medical insurance that are subscribed to outside the university's benefits network; domestic partner benefits; tuition reimbursement; access to faculty/employee housing; career counseling; and employee assistance programs (see Chapter 6).

Library-Supported Benefits

Libraries can also make several additional benefits available. It is the human resource specialist's responsibility to be aware of benefits offered by other libraries to ensure that his or her own library is competitive. Some library-supported benefits have a financial component; others are considered to have a nonfinancial impact.

Financial Benefits

Benefits that have a financial component are in the form of either direct compensation or indirect compensation. Examples of direct compensation benefits are pay differentials for evening and weekend work, on-call pay, recognition awards, and retention bonuses.

Indirect compensation benefits include such things as breaks and leave time to attend conferences, workshops, for-credit course work, or departmental and library parties. Most academic librarians with faculty status are eligible for sabbatical leave per the parent institution's guidelines. In general, sabbatical leaves are for either one semester or one year, with compensation amounting to either full or half pay, respectively. For those employees who are not considered academic faculty eligible for regular academic sabbatical leaves, libraries can still accommodate a research agenda by offering leave with pay, much the same as a sabbatical. In fact, offering research leave is a common practice in academic libraries that require research to be a component in the work load.

According to Singer (2002), creating a work environment that is supportive of professional growth and participation is an important component of the total compensation package. Paid leave to attend conferences and workshops and to take course work is commonly part of a librarian's benefit package but can be unusual for support staff. However, providing paid leave to support staff for professional growth opportunities can build loyalty within the library and can strengthen employees' skill sets so they will be more valuable library workers.

Nonfinancial Benefits

Burnout and on-the-job stress are two by-products of library employees spending increasingly more time at work. In many cases, being "at work" does not necessarily mean physically being in the library. Many library employees routinely take work home on evenings and weekends. The human resource specialist should be aware of work- and life-enhancing programs such as the following:

- Flex time: Work hours are scheduled to allow for flexibility to work a schedule that is not the typical 8:00 to 5:00, Monday through Friday work week.

- Job sharing: Two part-time employees perform the work of one and share hours, job duties, and responsibilities.

- Flexplace/telecommuting: employees are allowed to work at home either full- or part-time. Many library jobs are not conducive to telecommuting, but as library work becomes more technology based, telecommuting is becoming more realistic for librarians.

- Compressed work weeks: Instead of working five eight-hour days, the employee might work four ten-hour days, four nine-hour days and four hours on one day, or any other combination that fulfills the work week hours.

- Part-time: Part-time work can be temporary or permanent and can be structured in many different ways, such as the traditional twenty hours per week job or full-time for the academic school year with summers off.

Other nonfinancial benefits include such concepts as wellness benefits like CPR and/or first aid training, stop smoking programs, and weight loss programs; staff development and on-the-job training programs; coaching/mentoring programs; career counseling; and leave to attend conferences and workshops.

Conclusion

Compensation plays a vital role in the recruitment and retention of both librarians and library support staff. Although significant increases have been made in the salary ranges and benefits generally provided to academic library employees, there is considerable room for improvement. The academic library human resource specialist can set in motion strategies that can be implemented to address salary inequities and improve the benefits package available to library employees. In a nutshell, two important concepts should be investigated: the strategic use of communication to build a more thorough understanding of and support for better salaries, and creating alliances with such organizations as unions, state library associations, and the American Library Association's Better Salaries/Pay Equity Task Force to advocate for better salaries.

Part of the total compensation package is benefits, both those traditionally provided by the parent institution such as health, life, and dental insurance; sick, vacation, and holiday leave; retirement plans; and the ability to contribute to a tax deferred annuity, as well as those offered by the library. Creating a work environment that is appreciative of its employees and conducive to professional growth is a critical part of the total compensation package. The human resource specialist must be knowledgeable of concepts such as work-life balance and what is valued by today's library employee.

Guidelines the human resource specialist should take into account when setting salaries and putting together a total compensation package include

Monetary factors, such as

- Consideration of the geographic area,
- Skills and knowledge needed for the position,
- The cost of living in the area,
- The level of duties and responsibilities of the position,
- Salary comparison with similar positions,

- Alternative pay plans (including pay differentials for weekend and evening duties),
- On-call pay,
- Recognition awards,
- Promotion opportunities, and
- Monetary support to attend conferences and workshops; and

Nonmonetary factors, such as

- Staff development/professional growth opportunities:
  Leave package
  Attendance at conferences and workshops
  Research leave
  Injury leave
  Workers' compensation leave,
- Flexplace/telecommuting,
- Flextime,
- Job sharing,
- Compressed work weeks, and
- Part-time option with benefit prorated.

There is no doubt that compensation and benefits are complicated and sensitive subjects. However, they are very important issues that cannot be overlooked by library administrators. As budgets decline and competition increases for library employees, library administrators are obligated to make a commitment to strategically address salaries and benefits.

References

Baker, Cathy A., and Iris S. Diaz. 2001. "Managed Plans and Managed Care Features: Data from the EBS to the NCS." *Compensation and Working Conditions* (Spring) 30–36.

Better Salaries/Pay Equity Task Force Mission. 2002. Available: http://www.mjfreedman.org/tfmission.pdf. (Accessed March 14, 2003).

Center for Policy Alternatives. 2002. *State Issues.* Available: http://www.stateaction.org/issues/workcompensation/livingwage/index.cfm. (Accessed March 14, 2003).

FastFacts. 2000, February 29. Denver: Library Research Service. Available: http://www.lrs.org/Fast_Facts.htm. (Accessed February 20, 2003).

Fisk, Donald. 2001. "American Labor in the 20th Century." *Compensation and Working Conditions Online* (Fall). Available: http://www.bls.gov/opub/cwc/cm20030124ar02p1.htm. (Accessed February 20, 2003).

Kyrillidou, Martha, and Mark Young. 2002. *ARL Annual Salary Survey, 2001–2002.* Washington, DC: Association of Research Libraries.

National Committee on Pay Equity. 2001. *The Wage Gap Over Time.* Available: www.feminist.com/fairplay/f_change.htm. (Accessed February 20, 2003).

Schwenk, Albert E., and Jordan N. Pfuntner. 2001. "Compensation in the Later Part of the Century." *Compensation and Working Conditions Online* (Fall). Available: http://www.bls.gov/opub/cwc/archive/fall2001art6.pdf. (Accessed February 20, 2003).

Seaman, Scott. 1999. "An Internal Equity Evaluation System Based on Merit Measures." *College & Research Libraries* 60, no. 1: 79–89.

Simpson, Hilery. 1997. "Paid Personal, Funeral, Jury Duty, and Military Leave: Highlights form the Employee Benefits Survey, 1979–1995." *Compensation and Working Conditions* (Winter): 35–46.

Singer, Paula. 2002. *Developing a Compensation Plan for Your Library.* Chicago: American Library Association.

Special Libraries Association. 2002. *2002 SLA Salary Survey.* Available: www.sla.org. (Accessed February 19, 2003).

Terrell, Tom. 2002. "Salaries Rebound, Women Break Out." *Library Journal,* 127 (October 15): 30–31, 36.

Terrell, Tom, and Vicki Gregory. 2003. "A Look at Now and Then: Salaries of Academic and Research Librarians." Presented at ACRL National Conference, Charlotte, NC, April 11.

Union Membership and Earnings Data Book. 2001. Washington, DC: Bureau of National Affairs.

United States Chamber of Commerce. 2003. *News Press Release* (January 21). Available: www.uschamber.com/press/releases/2003/January/03-13htm. (Accessed February 20, 2003).

Whittington, Glenn. 2003. "Changes in Workers' Compensation Laws, 2002." *Monthly Labor Review* (January): 25–29.

Academic Library Leadership: Meeting the Reality of the Twenty-First Century

Sheila D. Creth

Leadership: Myths and Reality

Research on Leadership and Leaders

Defining leadership has been the topic of numerous journal articles and books on the philosophy and characteristics of successful leaders as well as the role of leadership in a successful organization. The research on and discussion of leadership has spanned more than fifty years and remains an ever-present focus in addressing the success of organizations, particularly in a time of accelerated change and external pressures.

Although most of the leadership literature focuses on the traditional view of leaders and leadership, there have been significant shifts in perceptions of leadership over the past decade. One significant change is that leadership no longer is viewed as residing solely in top management positions. Instead, "distributed leadership" among various people and positions is considered the mark of a successful organization. The second change is the belief that leadership is not just demonstrated in relation to the major activities and goals of the organization; rather, leadership is expressed through different activities, projects, and quality service throughout the organization. Most important, there now is considerable attention focused on the development of individuals as leaders through various types of learning opportunities.

Mathews and Wacker, in their stimulating book *The Deviant's Advantage,* state that "the context of traditional leadership has been fatally compromised" (2002, 188). Although there has been considerable research into and assessment of leadership in the business literature, leadership in librarianship—as contrasted with management—has received minimal attention.

Karp and Murdock (1998) describe their experience in developing a bibliography on library leadership as "tedious" because they had to "pick through thousands of citations" under various subject headings since the word "leadership" was not used. They indicate that the lack of leadership as a subject heading may indicate an issue larger than one of access. "Leadership as a concept in the profession of librarianship seems not to be concretely acknowledged as a legitimate entity that merits clearly identified discussion and definition" (1998, 251).

Riggs asks, "why is there a dearth of articles and books on the topic of leadership in libraries?" (1998, 55). He goes on to state that leadership is important to the future of academic libraries as they face unprecedented change and are "continually reshaping themselves." Riggs believes that "the twenty-first century demands visionary leadership. It cannot function without it. Without a sense of urgency for action, a realistic and credible long-term plan, and the actual development of a compelling vision for the library's future, the academic library is a viable candidate for self-destruction" (1998, 65).

Academic librarians clearly need to broaden the view of their role and responsibilities to explore ways in which they can and should exercise leadership in the context of the library and the campus. And they urgently need to develop, and to help others to develop, leadership capabilities.

Myths About Leadership

Although no definitive definition or single set of behaviors has been identified in relation to leadership, it is possible to eliminate certain assumptions that create barriers to understanding leadership. Bennis and Nanus (1997), in *Leaders: Strategies for Taking Charge,* describe a set of myths regarding leadership that they claim discourage potential leaders. A review of these myths is helpful to expand one's understanding of who can exercise leadership specifically in the academic library. The five myths Bennis and Nanus identify appear frequently as absolutes in the leadership literature:

- Leadership is a rare skill.

- Leaders are born, not made.

- Leaders are charismatic.

- Leadership exists only at the top of an organization.

- Leaders control, direct, prod, and manipulate. (1997, 206–90)

Bennis and Nanus state that "everyone has leadership potential . . . leadership opportunities are plentiful and within the reach of most people." They also comment that "major capacities and competencies of leadership can be learned. . . . It is a deeply human process, full of trial and error, victories and defeats" (1997, 206–7).

Those who occupy recognized leadership positions should openly dispel these myths about leadership through education and training, so that individuals will be more likely to recognize their own capacity and opportunities for leadership.

Characteristics and Behavior of Leaders

Although there has not emerged a single definitive statement from the flood of studies, books, and articles regarding leadership, there is sufficient agreement on a range of characteristics and behavior that identify leaders and effective leadership.

In *The Leadership Engine: How Winning Companies Build Leaders at Every Level,* Tichy (1997) presents a set of characteristics and behavior demonstrated by leaders. He states that leaders

- Are avid learners.

- Have smart ideas and get them implemented.

- Help others to develop their own ideas.

- Hold strong values that everyone understands and is held accountable.

- Are energetic and work to create positive emotional energy in others.

- Make tough decisions, encourage and reward others who do the same.

- Communicate and teach. (1997, 18–20)

He also states that "winning" organizations teach leadership and restructure the organization to "get rid of bureaucratic nonsense." Bennis and Nanus identify the following as behaviors of leaders:

- Lead by pulling rather than pushing;

- Inspire rather than ordering;

- Create achievable, though challenging, expectations and rewarding progress toward them;

- Enable people to use their own initiative and experiences not constraining their experiences and actions. (1997, 209)

Peter M. Senge (1994), in *The Fifth Discipline: The Art & Practice of the Learning Organization,* focuses on characteristics of leadership to create and sustain a learning organization. Senge describes the "traditional" view of leaders as "deeply rooted in an individualistic and nonsystemic worldview. . . . leaders are heroes" and, therefore, in this context only a few exceptional men and women can be leaders. Senge argues that the "new view of leadership in learning organizations centers on subtler and more important tasks. In a learning organization, leaders are designers, stewards, and teachers. They are responsible for building organizations where people continually expand their capabilities to understand complexity, clarify vision, and improve shared mental models" (1994, 340).

These characteristics and behaviors of leadership can operate at all levels of an organization and among people filling nonmanagerial positions as well as those in management. Karp and Murdock put forward a set of characteristics attributed to leaders, many of which are found in the broader literature. Leaders were described as having a clear concept of goals; being dynamic and competent; and acting as facilitators, stewards of vision, and risk takers (1998, 252). Library literature also identified other adjectives that describe leaders, including charismatic, political, consultative, confident, intuitive, assertive and self-aware, flexible, persuasive, innovative and creative, and optimistic. From these collective descriptions of behavior and characteristics related to leadership, it is clear that most individuals are able to demonstrate many of these qualities.

Since academic libraries are not isolated from demands that require effective leadership, the challenge of how leadership will be demonstrated in the academic library is a viable issue requiring attention. Indeed, as the economic base of society has emerged as information and knowledge based, libraries and the corporate world have become more closely interrelated. To protect the interest of the academic community and provide innovative services, librarians must exercise strong leadership to play a central role in defining issues related to access and distribution of information.

Specifically, librarians need to be effective leaders within their own libraries and academic institutions, within networks and consortia, and in various professional organizations and political settings. Considering the dynamics of events that affect the worlds of publishing, information access and control, and higher education, there is an urgency for librarians to exercise leadership in various ways as a primary tool for responding to the realities of the environment in which they exist. The strengthening of leadership within academic libraries is crucial to avoid self-destruction as greater complexity occurs in the academic library environment (Riggs 1998, 65).

Distinguishing Leadership and Management

The relationship between management and leadership is often confusing and confused, and many writers use the terms interchangeably. This is why much of the leadership literature focuses on individuals who occupy the CEO or other top positions in organizations rather than exploring leadership demonstrated by individuals in nonmanagerial positions.

Although management capabilities remain a significant need in an organization, the knowledge and skills and expectations are not the same as those for leadership. Nor is quality management sufficient to ensure success in achieving the organization's success. Leadership in partnership with management is required.

Unfortunately, there is a lack of agreement in the literature distinguishing the roles, contributions, and capability of managers and of leaders. In Rost's 1991 book on leadership, he includes a chapter addressing the relationship between management and leadership. He contrasts their roles as follows:

Leadership	Management
Influence relationship	Authority relationship
Leaders and followers	Managers and subordinates
Intend real changes	Produce and sell goods and/or services
Intended changes	Goods/services result from coordinated
reflect mutual purposes	activities (1991, 111)

In the decade since this book was published, the role of management has shifted away from a dependence on authority to focusing on persuasion and influence, and away from the traditional relationship to "subordinates."

Certainly in academic libraries, individuals occupying an administrative or department head position are not likely to be successful either within the library or on the campus by relying on authority as a way to achieve goals. Nonetheless, although there is a difference in the roles of managers and leaders, these are not exclusive but interdependent.

Kouzes and Posner (1997), in *The Leadership Challenge,* suggest a distinction between management and leadership based on the meaning of the root words "lead" and "manage." They describe the word "managing" as having at its "core" the handling of things—maintaining order, organization, and control, whereas "leading" has as its root the meaning to "go, travel, guide." Leaders, they say, go "first. They're pioneers. They begin the quest for a new order. They venture into unexplored territory" (1997, 36)

This distinction is helpful, because as others have pointed out, managers' responsibility is to achieve specific goals. Managers "tend to view work as an enabling process involving some combination of people and ideas interacting to establish strategies and make decisions. Furthermore, managers continually need to coordinate and balance opposing views. . . . [They] aim to shift balances of power toward solutions acceptable as compromises among conflicting values" (Zaleznik 1992, 128–29) Leaders, Zaleznik argues, work in "the opposite direction. . . . [They] develop fresh approaches to long-standing problems and open issues to new options. To be effective, leaders must project their ideas onto images that excite people and only then develop choices that give those images substance" (129). Tichy draws less of a distinction between the management and leadership responsibilities in an organization. He describes leaders as those who "determine direction, move organizations from where they are to where they need to be" (1997, 23). His expectation for leadership includes those in management.

Despite this separation of managers and leaders, and the need for managers to more often than not seek stability, compromise, and focus on achieving current goals, there is nothing inherent in the role of a manager—director or department head—that limits the individual in such a position from exercising leadership. More important, managers can encourage and develop leadership capacity among their own staff. The important distinction is that leadership is not restricted to or limited by one's managerial or administrative position. Leaders in an organization —including academic libraries—accept challenges, anticipate problems, and seize opportunities. In this way, they shape the future of the library rather than, through passivity, allowing the future to be defined by individuals and events external to the library.

Changing Expectations for Leadership

Leadership expectations and requirements have altered significantly over the past decade. Prior to this period, leaders were more often viewed as forceful managers who showed profitability and/or stability in the company products and services. In the academic setting, university presidents and academic officers were expected to focus internally on recruitment and retention of quality faculty, ensuring the attraction of quality students by offering a sound curriculum and potential for placement in top graduate programs or good positions upon graduation. The focus was on building solid, dependable programs—a future built on past success.

This is no longer the reality for those in top positions in the academic environment. University and college presidents are expected to be major fund raisers, to demonstrate sound political skills with alumni, corporations, and elected officials locally and nationally, all the while providing strategic leadership and commitment to academic excellence on the campus. This shift in expectations for leadership is not limited to presidents and central administrative academic officers but exists as well for others in the campus environment, including academic library directors.

Tichy and Devanna, in *The Transformational Leader*, describe three aspects of the organization needing particular attention from leaders in times of change: *technical, political, and cultural* (1986, 49). The *technical* aspects involve determining methods for achieving strategic planning and goal setting along with the management of the organization through periods of intense change. The *political* aspect relates to the more informal and often more influential process of how decisions are actually made, what tangible and intangible rewards and benefits operate, and what behaviors and results will be rewarded. The political aspect also covers relationships outside the organization.

Finally, Tichy and Devanna believe that leaders need to give attention to the *culture* of the organization to ensure that the appropriate values exist and are encouraged, new values are cultivated, and ones that are no longer relevant are minimized. This aspect of an organization is the most difficult to respond to because values operate on a conceptual basis and frequently are not apparent. Nonetheless, leaders need to spend time developing and cultivating values that are accepted and respected and that move the organization forward to the desired future.

Another significant change in expectations for leaders is their responsibility to address the growth and development of others—to create, in Senge's view, the "learning organization." He defines this type of organization as one "where people continually expand their capacity to create the results they truly desire, where new and expansive patterns of thinking are nurtured, where collective aspiration is set free, and where people are continually learning how to learn together" (1994, 3).

To achieve the learning organization, leaders—no matter where they are in the organization—need to view the development of people as the foundation for the library's future. They understand that people need to learn more than specific knowledge and skills to perform effectively in a highly changing and charged environment. Leaders also understand that people seek to belong, to build a commitment to their work and to their colleagues, and they wish to take pride in their work. Leaders attempt to respond to both the tangible and intangible development of individuals.

There are many ways to support and enhance the development of staff. It is the mark of a leader and a successful organization that the development of all staff is a top priority. This shift in expectations regarding what constitutes leadership has resulted in a broader understanding of who can and should exercise leadership.

Leadership Capacity in the Organization

Leadership as an activity and a responsibility should be seen in the broadest terms. Leadership viewed as occurring along a continuum demonstrates how different individuals can assume leadership roles and responsibilities. Some individuals might have an ongoing leadership role (e.g., the library director), while others might assume leadership responsibility based on specific activities (e.g., working on a project to develop an information literacy program). The concept of a continuum across which leadership is exercised in an academic library is to encourage individual staff members to recognize how they can act as leaders and, therefore, build leadership capacity as a means of strengthening the library. (See Figure 10.1, page 106.)

What is most important is to dispel the assumption—or myth—that leadership is restricted to those occupying administrative or department head positions. This is a view of leadership that limits this activity to only a select few. Such a view can be crippling to an organization. It is not possible for only a few people in the organization to understand or recognize where improvement or change is needed, or to have a full range of ideas to consider in addressing a broad range of issues and/or problems, or to see opportunities that might exist for innovative approaches in delivery of services.

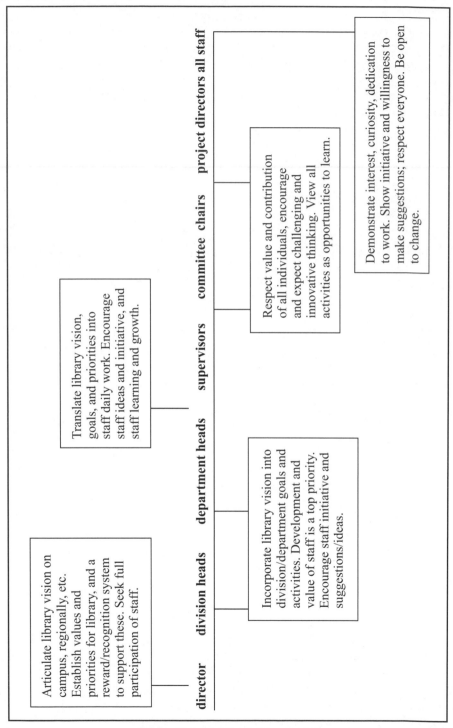

Figure 10.1. Distributed Leadership

The most successful organizations value each individual's leadership contribution within his or her area of responsibility and knowledge. Such organizations tend to be the most flexible in responding to change and difficult situations because more staff take an active role and responsibility for not only their own immediate work but also the organization's future.

Library Leadership Responsibility

If library organizations are to adapt and excel in the constantly changing information and academic environment, leadership should be legitimately exercised at multiple levels and by staff throughout the organization. While the director of the library and other administrative/managerial staff have a mandate, as integral to their responsibilities, to provide leadership, this activity cannot rest solely with these individuals. Instead it is desirable that a variety of people in different situations exercise leadership regarding their departmental goals and the broader mission and goals of the library. It is particularly important for library professionals to demonstrate leadership regardless of their position. Although the practice of shared leadership is not new in libraries, it has to date occurred only informally because there are always individuals who are willing to exert leadership within and beyond their specific position assignment.

What is required to expand leadership is the establishment of an organization norm that encourages all staff to demonstrate leadership appropriate to their roles, responsibilities, knowledge, and skills. Such expectations move toward ensuring that the full capacity of staff talent and energy is brought to bear on the many challenges facing the academic library.

Distributed leaderships also means a departure from staff expecting that all decisions rest with the administrative staff to an expectation that they will share in and accept responsibility for the directions and results of specific goals and the overall mission of the library.

It might be helpful to consider shared leadership in relation to the concept of participatory management. *Participatory management* is based on the view that aspects of management responsibilities could be shared—that is, *how* the organization implements what is envisioned for the future through planning, allocation of resources, and policy development could and should involve staff other than those in library management positions. In contrast, *shared leadership* suggests that multiple people have value to contribute in shaping *what* the library will become by identifying innovative and imaginative services, building and maintaining sound relationships on campus, and taking personal responsibility for the overall mission and vision of the library.

Library Director As Leader

Expectations of how academic library directors will participate in the academic environment has changed considerably. The library is no longer the bastion of quiet contemplation or gentlemanly agreements. Indeed, the academic library may be the focus of tension and stress related to what faculty members want for the collections, while also being a place of visibility and excitement in the integration of new technologies for broadening access to information resources. Leadership by the library director has a direct impact on the value and belief among campus administrators and faculty that the library is fundamental to quality teaching, research, and independent learning. This in turn affects funding, partnerships, and opportunities for contributing to the quality of the institution.

Williams, in "The Library Director as a Campus Leader," says that "there is no doubt that the library has a place in the university of the future, but it is less clear what that place will be. . . . The library director must be both an active and an effective advocate for the library on campus and a full participant in the life of the academic community." Williams believes that library directors must function as "part of a team consisting of college deans, faculty leaders, technical professionals, and members of the central administration to bridge the gap between traditional values and advancing technology" (1998, 42–43).

Of course, library directors are not always perceived by their campus colleagues as being part of the academic team—they are not always "invited to the party." Leadership requires that the library director take the initiative to become part of the team. Williams states that the library director must "actively seek out opportunities for collaboration with others on campus . . . inserting the library's influence and expertise in places where they can be used to advantage." He goes on to state that the library director—and the staff—should understand who the "key leaders for change will be on the campus and place themselves among that group" (1998, 49). Therefore, the library director needs to ensure that he or she is providing active, energetic, and visible leadership within the library and on the campus prior to expecting library staff to assume leadership responsibility.

At the same time, library directors and other library administrators cannot afford to be either parochial or possessive in shaping the library's future; if they are they may find themselves alone in trying to reach that future. Instead, shared leadership represents an opportunity to instill and maintain vitality and creativity in all aspects of library operations and services. To involve the library's nonmanagerial staff in assuming leadership responsibility, the library director must offer clear and enthusiastic support for this expectation and articulate ways in which distributed leadership might be demonstrated by staff throughout the organization. The library director is key in setting the tone for the library, articulating a value for contributions by all staff based on their knowledge and abilities (rather than on their positions), and again ensuring that the recognition and reward system supports the new expectations. In addition, the director will need to work closely with other library administrators and department heads to set expectations for sharing leadership and creating an open and learning organization, as well as providing staff opportunities for leadership development. Finally, academic library directors should be critical in assessing their behavior to determine whether they are in fact acting as a model by sharing leadership responsibilities with others.

Librarians As Leaders

Leadership depends not only on the administrative staff relinquishing their hold on leadership by creating a more open organization in which individual and team initiative and innovation is encouraged, but also on the willingness of individual staff members to accept this responsibility. Most particularly, the librarians and/or professional staff of the academic library have a fundamental responsibility to provide leadership and direction in shaping the future of the library. In general, there is an expectation of outreach to all the constituents served, such as faculty, students, and the larger community, plus an expectation to consider and implement new approaches and ideas in services while maintaining the familiar traditional activities of the library. For example, librarians are no longer able to simply be in the library at a reference desk should a student or faculty member have a question. Now it is expected that librarians will initiate and seek out faculty and students to offer user education sessions so that individuals learn about library resources and how to access and evaluate these resources. Librarians also are expected to work more cooperatively and in conjunction with faculty and academic departments in developing services and seeking funding to expand or initiate new services. In addition, librarians are expected to seek ways to cooperate with other libraries in their state and/or region to expand access to resources for their immediate constituents. This broader involvement in cooperative ventures requires leadership from various librarians to shape services in new and different ways and to reach agreement on complex issues.

Williams indicates that "librarians must participate in planning for the use of electronic technologies on campus, work collaboratively with computer professionals and others on campus, retrain staff, secure funding for both infrastructure development and operations, understand intellectual property issues and learn to work in an environment in which change is a constant" (1998, 42). Furthermore, he believes that librarians—not only library directors—"must gain the trust of those who make decisions for the campus and must work with others in the library to constantly renew, modify, and/or redefine the values and goals in the libraries so that they stay within the changing priorities of the institution" (1998, 49). If librarians accept this as part of their responsibilities, then they are accepting a leadership role.

All Staff As Leaders

Although librarians and library administrators have a very specific and professional responsibility to exercise leadership, all staff members can be encouraged and rewarded for assuming greater responsibility for the quality and overall effectiveness of their work. When a library assistant asks, "Why do we do this?" the answer should never be "because we always have." This is an opportunity for both the library assistant and the supervisor to answer the "why" and to demonstrate initiative in examining whether what is being performed is necessary and organized in the best possible manner. In all regards, staff should be given far more latitude to make decisions, to raise questions, and to suggest new approaches regarding their work and the work of the department. Quite often in academic libraries, in particular, library staff in various positions are well educated and experienced, and they have ore ideas to contribute than may be acknowledged. (See Figure 10.2.)

In considering distributed and shared leadership, an organization cannot have everyone pulling in opposite directions and expect to move forward. The challenge for library administrators is to establish a balance between their managerial and leadership responsibilities and those of staff to play an active role in defining library directions and innovative services. Leadership at the top of the organization has a responsibility to describe the vision and directions and then involve others in refining this vision, and then identify an organizational design, values, and reward/recognition system that will support expanded leadership and staff involvement throughout the organization.

Organizing for Effective Leadership

In many academic libraries, it may not be sufficient to declare that leadership exercised by nonmanagerial staff is desired. It may be necessary to alter the basic organization of the library to remove barriers and to facilitate ways in which all staff members can interact and work more openly and effectively together and thus demonstrate leadership. To provide opportunities for individuals and groups to take on the role of leaders, consideration should be given to creating and encouraging more fluid and spontaneous working relationships among library staff. Nadler and Tushman observe that "the only real, sustainable source of competitive advantage lies in an organization's 'architecture'—the way in which it structures and coordinates it people and processes in order to maximize its unique capability over the long haul" (1997, viii).

Director
- Describe the vision/future for the library that articulates the library's central role in relation to academic mission and strategic plan. Work with staff to gain acceptance of the vision.
- Promote the vision on campus through active participation in various campus administrative meetings, and individual meetings with deans, academic department heads, and influential campus leaders.
- Seek campus partners to achieve the vision, and the necessary funding to support it. Provide an energetic and ambitious plan for support of library goals.
- Encourage an active and innovative role for library staff in meeting challenges and delivery of services, and establish a recognition and reward system to support them.
- Support the development of staff, including their leadership capabilities.

Reference Department Head
- Promote and incorporate the library vision/mission into division and/or department goals and activities. Ensure that this is the framework for determining department and individual priorities.
- Provide frequent opportunities to obtain staff ideas, and encourage staff to take the initiative in their contacts with faculty and students in developing innovative approaches to service.
- Reward and recognize individuals and teams for innovation and leadership.
- Provide learning opportunities for staff in various settings.

Circulation Supervisor
- Through initial and ongoing training, focus on the vision, goals, and priorities of the library and the relationship of each individual's work to the overall mission.
- Encourage staff to contribute ideas on procedures and policies, and be open to changes suggested by staff.
- Support and make time for continuous learning by staff.

Committee Chairs and Project Directors
- Establish high expectations for individual contributions, open discussion, critical analysis, and respect for each individual.
- Recognize the learning potential in all activities and ensure full participation of all staff.

Branch Library Assistant
- Take responsibility for quality of work and take the initiative to make suggestions regarding all aspects of work to ensure quality
- Be open to change and learning new practices, technologies, etc.
- Represent the library mission, vision, and values in all interactions with colleagues and users.

Figure 10.2. Examples of Leadership Behavior

Culture and Leadership

When considering how to ensure organizational success through expanding leadership, it is critical that culture not be overlooked. Schein warns that in managing culture in the organization, "the biggest danger you face is that you do not fully appreciate the depth and power of culture" (1999, 185). Schein describes culture as comprising espoused values (strategies, goals, philosophies) and basic underlying assumptions (belief, perceptions, thoughts and feelings), which are the ultimate source of values and action (1999, 16). He explains that culture is stable and difficult to change "because it represents the accumulated learning of a group—the ways of thinking, feeling and perceiving the world that have made the group successful" (1999, 21). The understanding of values—often not even explicitly acknowledged—is learned by new members of the organization as they work and interact with others. Experience teaches them what is acceptable and unacceptable in terms of behavior within the organization.

The culture of the organization is important, then, if there is to be a change in how leadership is perceived and implemented. If indeed there is a desire for a distributed leadership, then the imbedded values in the culture will have to be examined and addressed to ensure that a stated expectation for staff to exercise leadership does not conflict with existing values that are strongly held.

For example, many libraries have a culture rooted in a tradition of authority located at the top of the organization's hierarchy. In this environment, staff understand what is expected of them—what is valued: that they do their work as instructed, that they follow directions as given, and that they do not make changes without permission.

If there is a desire to have librarians and other staff members exercise leadership—to show initiative and take responsibility for shaping the library's future by thinking in an innovative way about services and programs—then it is necessary to address the culture and the values imbedded in the culture. It will not be sufficient for the library director and others to simply announce that they value and expect innovation and initiative from staff. Instead they will need to work with staff to identify any existing values or behavior that might create a barrier to people acting on this expectation.

Tichy says "changing people's values is even harder than changing their ideas, but in the long run it is probably more important" (1997, 127). He points out that values provide a "shared understanding that allows people to act independently . . . to design their own actions by defining the rules of behavior and establishing the forms of conduct that will be rewarded, or not tolerated" (1997, 106). So new or different values may be needed in the academic library to promote a distributed leadership capacity.

Organizational Design to Encourage Leadership

Although there has been considerable discussion and review of the traditional academic library organization in the past decade, much remains to be done to reduce the rigidity and formality of the hierarchical approach and to introduce greater flexibility to increase innovation and initiative among staff throughout the organization. There is no "one way" to organize the academic library. The reality of a particular academic institution and library should provide the framework for selecting options for redesign of the organization. And when major changes in the culture and the organization are contemplated, this should be accompanied by clearly stated expectations and values, an appropriate recognition and reward system, and staff development opportunities to reinforce the new culture and expectations and to provide learning of new knowledge and skills.

As a first step in considering organizational design, the difference between *organizational structure* and *processes* should be understood. They are interrelated, and both are essential in sustaining a viable and responsive organization; it is important to recognize how each contributes to organizational effectiveness.

The organizational *structure* defines how work responsibilities are assigned and the way in which departments are organized to get work accomplished. The structure provides clarity regarding individual and group responsibility both for employees and those who are served by the organization. The structure is the formal aspect of the organization and is the basis for stability. The *processes* of an organization provide the context for how people accomplish their work within the established structure. These processes consist of working relationships, communication systems (formal and informal), and interdependence among groups and individuals. The organizational processes are where the greatest flexibility resides.

It is possible for a traditional hierarchical library structure with divisions (e.g., public and technical services) and departments (e.g., reference, interlibrary loan, etc.) to coexist with distributed leadership by emphasizing new processes such as creating teams that draw on people from different departments to institute new or revised services. When such a team is given the authority and responsibility to develop a new program, then the members of the team will be able to exercise shared leadership. For this to actually work, however, the values within the library must be examined, as must the processes for recognition and reward, to make sure they are aligned with the stated expectations for leadership.

Bennis and Nanus suggest that organizations may be "learning handicapped" but that they can be redesigned to create "*open organizations* that are both *participative* and *anticipative*" (1997, 195). In this redesigned open organization, "people share a set of norms, values, and priorities that contribute to learning—alertness to change, a search for new challenges and options, and respect for innovation and risk taking"(195).

Even if the culture and organizational structure and processes have been addressed, individual members of the organization will have to commit to changes in their own approaches to work and working relationships and demonstrate a willingness to adopt new behavior and values. It is not enough for library administrators to change; all participants in the academic library should assume active responsibility for a shift to a more participatory and distributed leadership organization.

In academic libraries this means that the recognition and reward system has to support these new expectations, and the recruitment and selection of individuals for all positions will be based on new values and expectations. In addition, the role of administrators and department heads will have to change. Although many, if not most, academic libraries may maintain a hierarchical structure to coordinate major decisions such as allocation of resources, strategic planning, priority setting, and a variety of personnel policies, the administrative staff must be willing to let go of absolute control to create an open organization that encourages learning and distributed leadership (see Table 10.1). The challenge for academic library directors and their staffs is how to create a balance of stability and flexibility throughout the organizational structure and processes.

Table 10.1 Likely Model of Twenty-First-Century Leadership

From	To
Few leaders, mainly at the top; many managers	Leaders at every level; fewer managers
Leading by goal-setting	Leading by vision, creating new directions for long-term growth
Downsizing, benchmarking for low cost, high quality	Creating domains of uniqueness, distinctive competencies
Reactive/adaptive to change	Anticipative and creative
Designer of hierarchical organization	Designer of flatter, distributed, more collegial organizations
Directing and supervising	Empowering and inspiring and facilitating team work
Information held by few	Information shared with many
Boss	Coach
Stabilizer, balancing conflicting demands and maintaining culture	Change agent, balancing risks and evolving the culture
Developing good managers	Developing future leaders

Adapted from Bennis and Nanus, 1997, 217.

The greatest opportunity for success in any academic library lies with the staff. As one colleague observed, our most valuable resource goes home every night. The power of the staff can be magnified if the organizational structure and processes, along with the culture, are reviewed and revised, and distributed leadership and the development of effective leaders become a library value and a priority.

References

Bennis, Warren, and Burt Nanus. 1997. *Leaders: Strategies for Taking Charge.* 2d ed. New York: HarperCollins.

Creth, Sheila D. 1988. "Organizational Leadership: Challenges Within the Library." In *Leadership for Research Libraries.* Edited by Anne Woodsworth and Barbara von Wahlde. Metuchen, NJ: Scarecrow Press.

Creth, Sheila D. 2000. "Optimizing Organization Design for the Future." *Educause Quarterly* 23, no. 1 (April): 32–38.

Karp, Rashelle S., and Cindy Murdock. 1998. "Leadership in Librarianship." In *Leadership and Academic Librarians.* Edited by Terrence F. Mech and Gerard B. McCabe. Westport, CT: Greenwood Press.

Kouzes, James M., and Barry Z. Posner. 1997. *The Leadership Challenge: How to Keep Getting Extraordinary Things Done in Organizations.* San Francisco: Jossey-Bass.

Mathews, Ryan, and Watts Wacker. 2002. *The Deviant's Advantage: How Fringe Ideas Create Mass Markets.* New York: Crown.

Nadler, David A., and Michael L. Tushman. 1997. *Competing by Design: The Power of Organizational Architecture.* New York: Oxford University Press.

Riggs, Donald E. 1998. "Vision Leadership." In *Leadership and Academic Librarians.* Edited by Terrence F. Mech and Gerard B. McCabe. Westport, CT: Greenwood Press.

Rost, Joseph C. 1991. "Leadership and Management." In *Leadership for the Twenty-First Century.* Westport, CT: Greenwood Press.

Schein, Edgar H. 1999. *The Corporate Culture Survival Guide: Sense and Nonsense About Culture Change.* San Francisco: Jossey-Bass.

Senge, Peter M. 1994. *The Fifth Discipline: The Art and Practice of the Learning Organization.* New York: Doubleday—Currency Paperback.

Tichy, Noel M. 1997. *The Leadership Engine. How Winning Companies Build Leaders at Every Level.* New York: HarperCollins.

Tichy, Noel M., and Mary Ann Devanna. 1986. *The Transformational Leader.* New York: Wiley.

Williams, Delmus E. 1998. "The Library Director as a Campus Leader." In *Leadership and Academic Librarians.* Edited by Terrence F. Mech and Gerard B. McCabe. Westport, CT: Greenwood Press.

Zaleznik, Abraham. 1992. "Managers and Leaders: Are They Different?" *Harvard Business Review* (March–April): 126–35.

Changing Roles of
Academic Librarians

Janice Simmons-Welburn

What do human resource administrators need to think about concerning the nature of work in academic libraries, and in particular the composition and role of staff? There is ample evidence that the past two decades of restructuring, reengineering, and organizational redesign in academic libraries, when combined with changes in the delivery of information and instruction, have all transformed library human resource management. This chapter explores the implications of these changes by reviewing recent literature on changing roles of library professionals and the value of relevant themes from the sociology of professions. Expectations of both libraries and library professionals are then reviewed, followed by consideration of the implications for planning and implementing human resource programs.

Background

Several factors have led to changes in the role of professional staff in libraries. With a migration toward more flattened organizational structures, more academic libraries have begun to adopt team leader and coordinator models in the place of traditional hierarchies. An increase in the use of new technologies to deliver and expand services has necessitated an enhanced skill set that meshes knowledge of new and emerging technologies. The desire to utilize electronic resources and to develop Web portals has also profoundly affected collection development (Casserly 2002, 583) by requiring more Web development competency among collection developers and bibliographers.

A significant number of published studies of employment patterns in academic libraries have attempted to define new requirements and expectations of library professionals. An Association of Research Libraries (ARL) report found through a careful review of job announcements from member libraries that "the changing roles of librarians and other professionals in ARL libraries are the consequence of new technologies and organizational development" (Simmons-Welburn 2000, 9). New positions were associated not only with technology, networked environments, information systems, and digital libraries, but also with a number of administrative professional positions resulting from organizational redesign. Representing a shift from traditional library skills, many new positions include budget and development officers, digital archivists, Web developers, application support programmers, and data librarians.

The ARL study also reported that "172 (or 25%) existing librarians' positions and 90 (or 44%) administrative positions were radically redesigned" (Simmons-Welburn 2000, 9) and that "a significant number of the descriptions collected indicated that the positions have been redefined to fit within new or reengineered organizational configurations. In some cases, new positions have emerged from organizational redesign and development" (Simmons-Welburn 2000, 10).

Stanley Wilder's research on demographic changes among academic library personnel has shown that the present and forecasted wave of retiring librarians has given many library administrators an opportunity to redesign positions around new requirements. The shift "represents a movement away from traditional library skills and library education generally. One is left with the overpowering sense that while the individuals who are about to leave this population may be replaced, their skills and professional training may not" (Wilder 2000, 5).

Several important studies conducted by Beverly Lynch documented changes in the stability of job requirements in academic libraries in the last three decades of the twentieth century. Whereas her research from the 1970s found relative stability in job requirements signaling traditional bureaucratic organization, a migration has occurred over the past twenty-five years that reflects responses to changing environment and organization, a shift from reliance on specific technical skill sets to such behavioral characteristics as flexibility and creativity, and the importance of continuous learning and professional development among library professionals. And while the MLIS continued to be a prerequisite for employment for most professional positions, there are expectations of an expanded knowledge base and a willingness to embrace organizational change:

> The specific emphasis on good communication skills emphasizes the growing importance libraries are placing on information services, instructional tasks, and interactions with patrons. The requirements for these skills do not negate the need for a professional knowledge and base in content; the required master's degree in LIS is the shorthand requirement for these. What these requirements for communication skills

emphasize is the need for library professionals to be able to interact with library patrons in many different ways. (Lynch and Smith 2001, 13)

As types of positions in academic libraries change, so have the selection criteria and requirements articulated in position descriptions. The distinction between public services versus technical services versus collection management is becoming less clear.

According to the ARL study, selection criteria for a reference position in one ARL library listed "client-centered service ethic" as a desired qualification. Another library stressed preferred experience working in a team environment; a position description for an Information Consultant and Coordinator of Distributed Learning and Electronic Resources included "demonstrated experience in negotiating licenses in an academic environment," and yet another pointed to "commitment to the realities of services." Yet another asked for a second graduate degree and Webmaster certification or site design certification (Simmons-Welburn 2000, 9).

Much of the research has relied on analysis of position descriptions or published job advertisements that have appeared in various venues read by academic librarians, and as such they emphasize the expectations of employers. However, it will be argued here that human resources administrators need to consider how academic libraries will strike a balance between what libraries can expect from the legions of new and continuing employees and, in particular, library professionals, and what organizations are willing to contribute to the professional development of their employees.

Academic Librarians and the Sociology of Professions

Academic libraries are distinguished by the people who work in them and the tasks that they perform. As part of professional bureaucracies, academic library staff are engaged in a kind and quality of intellectual teamwork mediating information and users with an array of information-seeking strategies. Academic libraries are also distinguished by staff that include librarians, technology specialists, and other professionals; support staff; and a large corps of student assistants seeking degrees at the very institutions the libraries serve. Given the range in background and expertise of academic library staff, it is pertinent to preface the implications of the changing roles by looking briefly at librarians as a professional group. As Andrew Abbott has argued, professional groups are defined by their relationship to a variety of societal factors: technology, organization, natural objects and facts, and cultural structures. According to Abbott:

> A profession is always vulnerable to changes in the objective character
> of its central tasks. . . . A task also has subjective qualities [that] may
> make it vulnerable to change . . . the subjective qualities of a task arise

in the current construction of the problem by the profession currently 'holding the jurisdiction' of that task . . . to investigate the subjective qualities of jurisdictions is thus to analyze the mechanisms of professional work itself. (1992, 145–46)

In other words, although academic library professionals may see changes occur in the way they perform tasks due to changes in technologies or in the policies of their parent institutions, other tasks performed in an academic setting by other professionals who hold jurisdiction over those tasks—including teaching and scholarly research—may also affect the way that academic librarians and other staff perform their work as well.

On the specific question the professional world of librarians, Abbott later wrote that librarianship "has always worked for organizations. It has always consisted of a loose aggregation of groups doing relatively different kinds of work but sharing a common orientation." Although one advantage of adaptability is being able to incorporate "current changes in work and organizations far more effectively than occupations like medicine," this adaptable nature also has its disadvantages. Essentially librarianship gives up its own exclusivity and autonomy in order to gain flexibility and the ability to adjust to changing environments. "Librarians too are used to relearning their jobs every decade or so, and that is in fact the paradigmatic experience in most professions" (1998, 441–42).

Recognizing and exploring those factors that influence the professional world of academic librarians is crucial to thinking about managing human resource issues and the organizational world of academic libraries. Much like the idea that a professional bureaucracy is closely associated with the capacity of the academic library to organize, the work of the federation of professions, together with support and student staffs, is also aligned with the ways in which people function in the workplace.

Given Abbott's view from the sociology of professions that libraries employ a federation of professions, and that such a federation is actually healthy for advancing library professionals, what patterns can be observed among the changes in libraries that are especially pertinent to managing human resources? Specifically, there are two sub-questions: What can libraries expect from their employees, and what can library professionals expect from their employers?

Patterns in Changing Responsibilities

As suggested by research, there are two patterns that emerge, that of increased technological abilities and managerial responsibilities. It is clear from these studies that MLIS programs are expected to underpin their curricula with technology so that graduates will be comfortable with the integration of various technologies with professional knowledge and skills. Recent LIS graduates are expected to be as comfortable with Web development and systems as they are with reference, collection development, and cataloging.

Likewise, there are a growing number of management responsibilities assumed by library professionals, including public relations and strategic communication, fundraising and development activities, assessment, and managerial skills development. All are crucial areas of development for LIS curricula geared toward responding to the needs of employees in libraries.

Yet what of mid-career librarians? Clearly, cooperation between LIS programs and libraries provides one model for continuing education. Still other approaches include in-house training by libraries and professional development programs offered by associations. The ARL/OLMS Online Lyceum Web-based courses are but one example of the use of distance education technology to meet the immediate needs of librarians. Professional associations are likely to have a crucial role in working with library professionals to upgrade knowledge in years to come (Greenwood, Suddaby, and Hinings 2002).

Library professionals can also expect that libraries will play an important role in promoting successful careers. In an article on the "new protean career contract," Douglas Hall and Jonathan Moss have suggested that the social contract between employees and employers that was at one time long-term and relationship-based is changing. "We are seeing a shift from the organizational career to what can be called the 'protean career,' a process which the person, not the organization, is managing. , , , If the old contract was with the organization, the protean contract is with the self and one's work" (Hall and Moss 1988, 25). Under this new contract, an employer worries more about continuous learning and advancing the career development of employees rather than rewarding their long-term loyalty to the organization. In the context of academic libraries, this means that library human resources administrators should worry less about whether an employee will spend her or his career in the same place and more about the employee's career and professional growth. In the long-run, such employees are likely to stay in an organization that invests in their future.

Implications for Human Resources

At least four implications for human resources administrators have been identified. Human resource managers will want to work with their organizations to integrate the ways in which change over the past several decades in academic libraries and their parent institutions, the environment for higher education, and the professional community of academic librarians affect not only recruitment of library professionals but also the entry of new employees into libraries as organizations. While a substantial body of literature has focused on recruiting to the profession, considerably less attention has been given to the arrival of new employees, what happens to them on their first day, the next day, and in the days and weeks following employment in a new organization. Specifically, a more concerted effort must be made to balance preservation of the individual identity of new employees with integration into the community as the practice of socialization proceeds for new employees.

Human resource managers will also need to maintain a commitment to continuous learning for all library staff through staff training and development. Such initiatives might not only include retooling veteran employees, especially those at mid-career, but also building in training for developing various managerial skills among those employees who supervise people, manage services and resources, and work externally with various clientele or constituents.

The redesign of organizations has moved libraries away from structures that operate or function like silos to ones that are more integrated and cross-functional. Given this, libraries will need to provide training on a continuous basis for all levels of staff so that they possess the necessary skills to effectively communicate and collaborate across the landscape of the organization. As libraries increase their emphasis on outreach and public relations, administrators and, in particular, human resource managers must ask what skills sets and training are needed to ensure success on the part of staff operating in different arenas. Likewise, assessment represents yet another area of increasing importance for academic libraries. As academic libraries place greater emphasis on outcomes in the face of shrinkages of resources, the need for assessment skill building becomes paramount.

Finally, academic libraries are likely to continue to experience a shift in the meaning of loyalty and, specifically, in understanding that employees remain with or leave organizations for a variety of reasons, some of which are out of the control of the library. Therefore, human resource managers will want to make a commitment to broaden responsibilities and opportunities. It is especially important to challenge new employees with an opportunity to grow and assume greater responsibility for professional work. At the same time, sensitivity to the increasing importance of the relationship between work and life is especially important for new library professionals, who perform their work to live rather than live for their work.

References

Abbott, Andrew. 1992. "Professional Work." In *Human Services as Complex Organizations,* 144–56. Edited by Yeheskel Hasenfeld. Newbury Park, CA: Sage.

Abbott, Andrew. 1998. "Professionalism and the Future of Librarianship." *Library Trends* 46 (January): 430–43.

Casserly, Mary Frances. 2002. "Developing a Concept of Collection for the Digital Age." *Portal: Libraries in the Academy* 2 (October): 577–87

Greenwood, Royston, Roy Suddaby, and C.R. Hinings. 2002. "Theorizing Change: the Role of Professional Associations in the Transformation of Institutionalized Fields." *Academy of Management Journal* 45, no. 1: 58–80.

Hall, Douglas T., and Jonathan E. Moss. 1988. "The New Protean Career Contract: Helping Organizations and Employees Adapt." *Organizational Dynamics* 26 (Winter): 22–37.

Lynch, Beverly P., and Kimberley Robles Smith. 2001. "The Changing Nature of Work in Academic Libraries." *College and Research Libraries* 62 (September): 407–20.

Simmons-Welburn, Janice. 2000, May. *Changing Roles of Library Professionals.* ARL SPEC Kit 256. Washington, DC: ARL.

Wilder, Stanley. 2000. "The Changing Profile of Research Library Professional Staff." *ARL: A Bimonthly Report on Research Library Issues and Actions from ARL, CNI, and SPARC* nos. 208/209 (February/April). Available: http://www.arl.org/newsltr/208_209/chgprofile.html. (Accessed June 4, 2003).

12

Educating Leaders

Mark Winston

Introduction

Academic libraries are operating in an era of increasing competitiveness, limited resources, a need for greater accountability to a number of stakeholders, and a technologically astute and demanding user population. While these broad issues have a direct impact on the human resources needs of libraries, organizational changes, such as greater use of teams in decision making and matrix organizational structures, have led to increasing complexity associated with managing human resources issues in academic libraries. The range and complexity of these HR issues, including the changing roles associated with shared leadership, greater communication challenges in team-based organizations, and evolving job descriptions, reflecting broad organizational considerations, influence the knowledge and skill sets required of new hires, the professional development needs of library faculty and staff, and the human resources issues associated with managing change in complex organizations. Thus, the range of human resources activities is represented by a number of broad areas of responsibility, such as leadership and coordination activities, data gathering, analysis, and decision making; advising; recruitment and retention, including issues of diversity; and professional development and training. The role of graduate education in preparing library professionals who possess an understanding of human resources issues in particular, and contribute to the success of their employing organizations in general, forms the basis for this discussion.

Graduate education provides a theoretical basis, as a part of what defines a true profession, in the context of practical examples, using instructional techniques that include lectures and demonstrations, case studies, simulations, and guest lectures. Graduate education should provide the opportunity to address a range of types of HR issues that students, as future professionals and administrators, are likely to encounter. Also, the issues can be addressed in context, in relation to the other courses in the curriculum, such that students understand diversity issues in relation to human resources, collection development, and user services, for example. Context also includes the consideration of human resources issues in relation to the broader philosophical constructs that underlie the nature of the profession, including intellectual freedom, intellectual property, and service, as well as the broader ethical and legal issues associated with human resources decisions. It seems that there could not be any greater value than preparing graduates who understand that, in the decisions made by librarians and the services provided, the work of information professionals takes place within a broader economic, social, political, and societal context.

The academic setting of the classroom also provides a "safe" environment for students to learn, test their ideas, and developing their skill sets, which is particularly important in relation to HR decisions, which, in the workplace, have repercussions that have a direct impact on the lives and livelihoods of people.

Human Resources in Academic Libraries

To provide the institutional context for the discussion of educational preparation associated with developing graduates of library and information science (LIS) programs who are able to understand and address HR issues, it is necessary to discuss the range of HR responsibilities in academic libraries. It is important to note that this discussion presumes that in some instances the coordination responsibilities in these areas are embodied in one position, particularly in larger research libraries. However, responsibilities for human resources activities are often dispersed among those in library administration. Also, some HR responsibilities fall to all supervisory and managerial library faculty and staff.

In academic libraries, the general coordination and leadership activities associated with HR include

- Leading HR planning and workforce development planning;

- The coordination of the work of search committees for open positions;

- The design and, in some instances, presentation of professional development training programs;

- The coordination of performance evaluation processes, including issues of compensation, pre-tenure, promotion and tenure, and post-tenure reviews, consistent with university guidelines and the unique faculty and professional responsibilities of librarians;

- The coordination of employee assistance and recognition programs;

- Maintaining liaison relationships with university HR and library and information science programs; and

- Representing the library in various circumstances internal and external to the larger institution.

The range of responsibilities involving data gathering, analysis, and decision making includes designing and conducting needs assessment surveys to identify professional development needs and collecting statistics regarding enrollment in and satisfaction with training. Other analytical activities include data gathering and analysis in relation to candidates recruited and interviewed for open positions; library staff and faculty demographics, as well as demographics of the profession in general; faculty and staff retention and turnover; and compensation and benefits among peer institutions, nationally, regionally, and by type of institution. Human resources responsibilities also include conducting research on and maintaining resources regarding areas of training and conducting research on and staying apprised of HR issues in the general management literature, higher education and nonprofit literature, and library and information science literature.

In addition, HR professionals in academic libraries serve as advisors and organizational experts on a range of other issues. For example, HR staff often ensure compliance with regulatory and statutory guidelines; advise employees of grievance procedures; facilitate conflict resolution processes; provide employee coaching and mentoring; and advise managers and administrators on a range of issues, such as sexual harassment, union and labor relations, EEO, and other diversity issues, such as recruitment, retention, and organizational climate.

In relation to recruitment and retention specifically, HR activities include the coordination of recruitment efforts for library faculty and staff positions; providing assistance in the development of job announcements; posting job ads; and ensuring that affirmative action, equal employment opportunity, and non-discrimination guidelines are communicated and followed.

Although there is a range of specific HR responsibilities, a number of key issues cut across these responsibilities and require consideration in providing further context and clarity in defining appropriate educational preparation for library professionals. These issues include analytical skills and decision making, ethics, and diversity.

Analytical Skills and Decision Making

As noted, a number of the HR responsibilities in academic libraries require analytical skills and effective decision-making abilities. This decision making requires the collection and use of data that represent HR activities, individual performance, overall organizational activities, performance, and compliance, as well as external benchmarks and demographics. Lance and Boucher have indicated the importance of the use of data in decision making in general, indicating that "academic library managers require a variety of data to inform their decision making. Such information ranges from general statistics, benchmarks, and performance measures to cost analysis results to data on a wide variety of specific topics, such as automated systems and networks, buildings, electronic access to information, fiscal trends, and salaries" (1996, 1). The data needed for sound decision making and a forward-thinking, informed approach to library management must be gathered from external sources, such as professional and scholarly organizations, government agencies, private sources, peer institutions, and published sources (1996, 1). In addition, data must be collected internally, reflecting organizational operations and performance and user evaluations. "Thus, there is the need for academic librarians to possess an understanding of data-gathering techniques, which are informed by an understanding of the nature of the research methodologies available, and an understanding of the statistical analysis techniques available, as well" (Williams and Winston 2003).

The published literature regarding LIS education includes discussion of a number of aspects of instruction related to research methods and statistics. However, the literature reflects the difficulty associated with incorporating this intimidating area of study into LIS education. According to Dilevko, there are a number of questions regarding how best to incorporate statistical analysis and research methods into LIS education, including "Should research methods be separated from statistics or not? Are there to be two courses or one? [and] Is the course to be taught within the LIS department, or is it to be outsourced to another department or faculty?" (2000, 307)

The need for effective methods of including research methods and statistics in LIS education programs is highlighted by the range of academic backgrounds of students in MLIS programs and the general anxiety associated with statistics and math. According to Dilevko, this issue is related to the fact that

> LIS programs attract students from a wide array of fields, many of which do not require research methods or statistics courses at the undergraduate level. Graduate students who have become accustomed to high levels of achievement and grades suddenly find themselves being introduced, often at great speed and with significant conceptual shortcuts, to a largely alien, mathematically based, and logic-driven discipline. (2000, 307)

The approaches for providing instruction related to research methods that have been addressed in the literature include the use of instructional approaches that focus on content, as well as "alleviating statistics anxiety" (Dilevko 2000, 310). Dilevko's proposed instructional methodology is "designed to decrease statistics and research methods anxiety by improving the perceived worth of statistics and by decreasing the fear of application of statistical principles" (2000, 310). The actual measurement of understanding of statistical methods presented in professional education is evidenced by performance in the workplace, particularly in relation to decision making that is supported by research and data.

Ethics

The need for leaders to exhibit integrity, particularly with regard to ethical decision making, has been highlighted in the general leadership literature, as well as in the literature of library and information science. In private sector research, the study of leadership competencies, the qualities, areas of knowledge, and abilities possessed by successful leaders, has focused on issues such as effective decision-making and communication skills. Integrity has also been identified as important, but as a competency that is difficult to measure (Intagliata, Ulrich, and Smallwood 2000). In library and information science, research considers the knowledge and abilities needed by leaders in academic libraries (Hernon, Powell, and Young 2002). A number of the "attributes" needed by academic library leaders relate to effective decision making, such as the ability to "think 'outside the box' (in new and creative ways applicable to the problem)," exhibiting "good judgment," making "tough decisions," and exhibiting integrity (Hernon, Powell, and Young 2002).

The need for ethical leadership is further supported by the number of challenges facing organizational leaders in the emerging environment, including the increased scrutiny of leaders and organizations by the media and a range of stakeholders, an increased emphasis on accountability, the growing number of competitors for libraries and information services, the proliferation of communication and information technology in the design and provision of information services, limited financial resources, and opportunities for ethical abuses.

In the case of human resources, there are additional and specific considerations in relation to the importance of ethics. For example, the processes of performance evaluation, employee counseling, sexual harassment, and conflict resolution require a particular focus on confidentiality and ensuring the development and maintenance of trust among all involved. In any instances in which employees must make decisions using information that is not available publicly, as is the case with many HR decisions, ethical considerations are of paramount importance. Much of the data gathered and used by those with HR responsibilities are subject to inclusion in legal proceedings, requiring adherence to ethical guidelines for pragmatic reasons associated with protecting the library and the larger institution from legal action. In addition, the nature of the decision making associated with HR issues, such as hiring and promotion decisions, compensation decisions, performance evaluations, and unfavorable personnel actions, requires, at the most basic level, fairness and integrity.

The importance of educating future leaders about ethics is reflected in developments in graduate programs in business. As educators in MBA programs have begun to place increased emphasis on ethics in their educational programs and to further consider how to do so, they have been motivated by a number of issues, following highly publicized cases of ethical abuses, such as Enron and Tyco. The educators make decisions based on an awareness of at least two major considerations affecting employers. First, organizational leaders understand that promoting ethical practices is pragmatic and is "good for business" ("Is Ethics Good Business?" 2003, 6–21), indicating the bases for decisions made by consumers and those who are making stock purchase decisions. There is also the emerging realization that graduates of MBA programs are concerned about the ethical track records and performance of companies when they make decisions about accepting offers of employment ("Graduates Drawn to Ethically Sound Companies" 2002, 295). Reflecting these considerations associated with organizational success and the employment decisions of graduates, business educators are re-emphasizing the importance of ethics in curricula in general (Hutchison 2002, 301–9; Richards, Gilbert, and Harris 2002, 447) and, quite understandably, in specific specialties, such as accounting (Armstrong, Ketz, and Owsen 2003, 1–16).

One specific ethical consideration focuses on issues of inclusion, equity, and fairness.

Diversity and Organizational Success

Diversity is a central component of HR management in libraries. However, it is necessary to consider the basis for the focus on diversity in academic libraries and the basis for implementing effective HR practices that contribute to the accomplishment of diversity-related goals.

Making diversity a priority in organizations is generally justified by the need to provide services for and recruit from the increasingly diverse population, as well as addressing past inequities and current unfairness and eliminating underrepresentation. However, recent research in the study of diversity in the private sector and to a limited extent in the academic environment, has also highlighted a connection between investment in diversity and overall organizational performance and success (Jasinowski 2001, 58–61). Managers and researchers realize that the reasons for promoting and fostering diversity within organizations go beyond the fact that it is a good thing to do. According to Koonce, "Now, companies are embracing diversity as a business focus and corporate value. Embracing diversity isn't just the right thing to do; there's a strong business case for it" (2001, 24).

In the study of organizational theory, researchers have documented that the companies that are the most diverse, as measured by factors such as minority employment at all levels, spending with minority suppliers, and underwriting business that goes to minority-owned investment banks, have also been identified as more successful companies overall (Colvin 1999, 53–54). Kuczynski reports similar results in her research, addressing what she has described as "a direct link between a company's leadership diversity [in particular, diverse representation among company leaders] and its stock market performance" (2002).

In providing an initial explanation for this relationship between diversity and organizational performance, Kuczynski notes, "Diverse leadership suggests that a company has drawn a wide pool of talent up through its ranks and is opening itself up to a variety of different views and ideas" (2002). This representation of diverse leadership includes the composition of the company's board and senior management, among other positions. Dean has shown similar results in relation to financial indicators of success being linked to having women in leadership roles specifically and greater diversity of perspectives in general. The research indicates that diversity-related goals, programs, and initiatives are the norm in many companies, as reflected in financial decisions (Schaeffer 2001, 62–66).

However, the relationship between diversity and organizational success is complex. Some studies have found a negative correlation between leadership diversity and organizational performance in the short term. The reasons for such changes in performance have included the difficulties associated with building consensus (Knight et al. 1999, 445–65). The research reflects the fact that differences in perspective create challenges associated with reaching consensus, overcoming traditional organizational cultures reflective of less diverse organizations, and organizational performance that is hindered, as organizational cultures change. Indeed, among the companies that have made substantial efforts to foster diversity and that have been the most successful companies overall, often the prevailing organizational culture had to be dismantled, with "a more inclusive one in its place" (Chen and Hickman 2000, 190).

Initial research regarding the course content in MBA and undergraduate business programs indicates that despite the recognition among corporate executives and organizational researchers of the relationship between diversity and organizational success, issues of diversity are addressed to a limited extent in MBA courses. Typically, issues of globalism and internationalism are addressed to a much greater extent (Winston 2002, 10), thus begging the question of the lack of educational preparation for graduates who are expected to contribute to the success of organizations for which diversity is a priority.

The limited study of leadership diversity in the academic environment has focused on women and racial minorities, with specific consideration of student populations. The research results have indicated that the colleges that are the most diverse are also the most highly rated, based on established rankings of academic and financial performance (Winston 2001b, 517–26). In addition, many university presidents have articulated the importance of fostering diversity to enhance the learning environment (McLaughlin 1999, 25–31; Rudenstine 1996, B1–B2).

The research into diversity in libraries focuses on issues of staffing, collections, services, and organizational climate (Winston and Li 2000, 205). Thus, diversity is a relatively broad issue, with a number of components that relate to human resources management, particularly in terms of staffing and organizational climate, in academic libraries, with specific areas of consideration, including recruitment, retention, and diversity training.

In many instances, library positions dedicated to issues of diversity have job titles and responsibilities that include, for example, a combination of staff development and diversity or human resources and diversity. The issues of staffing, both in terms of recruitment and retention, including the development of a diverse library staff, as well as the development of an understanding of diversity among library staff through training and professional development, are HR responsibilities. And, more than tangentially, issues of organizational climate, including morale, staff development, and managing organizational change, relate directly to HR. As the research has indicated, for organizations to realize the benefits of diversity efforts that are substantive in nature and that facilitate changes leading to organizational success, the prevailing organizational culture has to be dismantled and redesigned. The planning, recruitment, retention, training, coaching and mentoring, and conflict resolution that are likely to be a part of such organizational change are human resources responsibilities that must be addressed at many levels in organizations. Collections and services, as supported by diversity training and performance evaluation processes that consider contributions to the creation of an organization for which diversity is valued and promoted, are human resources issues as well.

Libraries in general and academic libraries in particular have made little progress in terms of diversity. Based on the relationship between diversity and organizational success, it is necessary for graduates to possess a sophisticated understanding of diversity issues, particularly as they address HR issues, to contribute to overall organizational success. Those

> professionals whose educational experiences have included education and learning about issues of race, gender, ability, orientation, the "-isms," and diversity are more likely to be in a position to apply their knowledge in the performance of their responsibilities and more likely to contribute to environments which foster diversity and to organizations which are successful. (Winston 2001a, 210)

It is important to note that, "In library and information science education, issues of diversity and multiculturalism are to be a part of the curricula of American Library Association-accredited master's programs" (Winston 2001a, 206). However, as Lorna Peterson has indicated:

> [T]he interpretation of this is left up to the individual library and information science school. A school can design a curriculum which does not address issues of equity, justice, and the historical difference in treatment of particular groups; a school can define diversity simply as the quality of being different and state that their graduates are prepared to work in a multicultural environment. (1999, 23)

The level of preparation that graduates receive about issues of diversity is likely to vary a great deal. Although researchers such as Welburn (1994, 329), Jeng (1997, 334), Peterson (1994, 24), Belay (1992, 299), and Winston (2001a,

199–212) have addressed instructional considerations and approaches to be considered in the incorporation of issues of diversity into the LIS curricula, the published research related to issues of diversity in libraries is limited (Welburn 1994, 329), with the result that the discussion of diversity that does occur in the LIS classroom is based largely on research in other disciplines or not supported by research at all.

In addition to the issues of curricular content, instructional approaches are important in increasing receptivity to diversity issues in the library setting. "Those professionals whose educational experiences also included learning in classroom settings, with instructors who utilized effective instructional techniques, which created comfortable, sensitive, yet dynamic learning environments, are likely to be more open to participating in discussions of issues of diversity in their workplaces" (Winston 2001a, 210).

Graduate Education

There is a need for a multi-pronged approach to ensure a well-developed understanding of human resources issues among those in the profession. The necessary components include graduate education, including internship experiences, as well as mentoring by knowledgeable librarians and administrators; in-house HR training in libraries; modeling of best practices; and development of a literature base that supports knowledge of HR challenges, developments, and best practices. A number of significant components of HR roles and responsibilities, such as ethics, analytical skills, and decision making, and diversity, are addressed here in relation to LIS education.

In a presentation at the Association for Library and Information Science Education Conference in January 2003, this author addressed the nature of LIS graduate education in the context of the expectations of professionals in the field. The presentation recounted the fact that a practitioner colleague had inquired as to whether the graduates of the LIS program of which the faculty member (this author) is a part are prepared for the first day of work in libraries when they graduate. The author's response was that a "yes-no" answer to the question is not appropriate because the question itself, to a large extent, misses the point—in this case, the point of graduate education. The fact is that graduate education is intended to provide a theoretical and conceptual basis, representing a more sophisticated understanding needed to support the decision making that follows in one's professional or academic career. Clarity is particularly important in the case of graduate education that is tied to preparation for professional practice, as opposed to graduate education in the arts and sciences, for example.

Subsequently, Robert Holley addressed this issue in *College and Research Libraries News*, indicating that

[T]he fundamental purpose of library education is not to train students for their first jobs but to prepare them for a professional career in librarianship. In addition to practical skills, students must acquire the ability to integrate new knowledge and become socialized to the values of the profession, such as open access, service, objectivity, and intellectual freedom. (2003, 173)

Certainly in the case of graduate programs in library and information science, one of the central goals is leadership preparation—that is, preparing graduates to take on leadership roles in their future careers and, more immediately, to understand their roles as professionals in supporting organizational leaders and contributing to organizational success. However, in a general sense, library and information science education must accomplish a number of ambitious goals, with a few distinct constraints in place. LIS education, as is the case with professional and graduate education in general, must address both the theoretical and the practical, fulfill accreditation standards, and do so with limited resources and within a limited number of course credit hours.

In the case of LIS education, there is a need to address a range of research, theoretical, practical, and philosophical issues in programs that require thirty-six to forty-two credit hours for graduation. In addition, the curricula of the programs must address a range of other content areas, including, among others, information technology (including searching and retrieval), organization, classification and cataloging, and reference and information services. This situation is particularly challenging because the programs recruit and admit students from a variety of undergraduate (and to a certain extent, prior graduate) educational backgrounds, including, most prominently, English and history, although that representation is changing somewhat. In the case of human resources management, few of the students have studied management in general or human resources issues in particular prior to entering LIS educational programs. Generally, there is no common theoretical base that students share. Thus, it is necessary to provide the theoretical and philosophical basis for issues such as intellectual freedom, intellectual property rights, and access to information, which supports so much of the decision making that allows those in the profession to fulfill our societal mission.

Although all of the ALA-accredited MLIS programs offer at least one management course (Winston and Hazlin 2003), a far smaller percentage (50 percent) require coursework in management for all students (Winston and Fisher 2003). Although it might be viewed as a potential difficulty that an even smaller percentage offer stand-alone HR courses, it might be argued that HR issues can be addressed in the context of courses with content that is more broadly focused but in which HR issues are relevant. The practical reality is that most LIS programs are not likely to offer elective courses in HR management. Thus, presumably, HR issues are most appropriately addressed in general management courses. While that does appear to be the case, the general management courses must address a range of other issues as well, including organizational theory, planning, organizational change, organizational communication, marketing and public relations, information technology, financial management, and measurement and evaluation.

In a general sense, it is necessary to note the importance of library and information science educators and practitioners being in communication regarding and collaborating in the educational preparation of LIS graduates. Certainly this type of communication is facilitated in a number of ways, including the participation of practitioners on advisory boards of LIS programs, as adjunct faculty, and as internship supervisors. Practitioners and educators, as well as the perpetuating factor of "too little interaction," need enhanced involvement to address the larger issue that Barbara Moran has suggested is such different perspectives, roles, and "masters" to be served. The premise is certainly that a lack of understanding appears to be the result.

In other disciplines, including business, nursing, and social work, there has been far more discussion of, though not always a greater number of examples of, educator-practitioner collaboration, focused specifically on enhancing the learning process for students (LeGris and Cote 1997, 55–70; Sawyer et al. 2000, 511–16; Stevens 1999, 151–62; Vest et al. 1997, 95–100).

Particularly among academic librarians, who understand the organizational constraints and the role of academic departments in supporting the educational and research mission of the larger institution and the need to prepare graduates who will represent the institution well, the support for graduate LIS education should be a high priority.

Further Preparation in HR Management

To build upon academic preparation received by graduates of MLIS programs, academic librarians should identify opportunities to offer internship experiences incorporating human resources issues, as a part of working in library administration or working in any other library department with supervisors or department heads, considering issues ranging from recruitment policies and conflict resolution to the supervision of student assistants. The opportunity for students to address practical issues with some theoretical understanding should be one of the hallmarks of a profession, as opposed to a trade, in that graduates understand not only the how-to-do-it but the why-to-do-it as well.

Whether students are working with academic librarians as interns or in student assistant positions, there is an opportunity for the development of beneficial mentoring relationships, such that student employees have a better understanding of the nature of library work and the roles of librarians, but also so that the student assistants understand that HR decisions are made, taking into account the big picture, in terms of organizational and unit mission, vision, and goals; the importance of services and user satisfaction; and overall employee contributions and well-being.

For classroom instruction, mentoring relationships, and internship and student assistant work experiences to be fully informed by the nature of professional practice, it is necessary for librarians and administrators to be consistent and thoughtful consumers of the research literature, to be aware of best practices. IAs the published literature serves as the basis for the theoretically grounded and research-based discussion of most issues in graduate educational programs, it is important that librarians contribute to the literature, presenting research results, often reflecting practice-based research, best practices, and perspectives gleaned from both unique and universal HR issues. Certainly, with unique cases not being disclosed, there are opportunities to address challenges, approaches, considerations, constraints, and learnings. Recruitment in general, and diversity in particular, are areas in which an understanding of best practices and the knowledge gained from research is relevant, based on the limited success in these areas in many libraries.

Ultimately, it is necessary for learning organizations that support the general concept of lifelong learning to provide in-house professional development training related to relevant human resources issues, providing the opportunity to address specific organizational considerations and, for example, the most recent legal developments for new and experienced librarians. Such professional development should build upon graduate educational preparation and be informed by the specific circumstances of the organizational context in question.

Conclusion

The challenges associated with educating and preparing LIS graduates are many, largely because much is expected of them when they accept professional positions in libraries, which face many challenges. This is particularly the case with HR issues, where the stakes are high, the livelihood of individuals is at the center, and emotions may run high as challenging decisions must be made. The individuals who are being prepared to address these issues come from more of a liberal arts tradition than an academic culture of studying and considering HR issues. In addition, both the complexity of HR issues and the philosophical and ethical issues underlying the decision making in academic libraries seem to require not only graduate educational preparation that is informed by theoretical underpinnings and the research base that define a true profession, as well as practical considerations and context and effective instructional approaches, but also the involvement of library professionals as program advisors, mentors, and internship supervisors. As partners in the academic enterprise, LIS educators and academic librarians understand and support the research and educational missions of their institutions and thus are logical collaborators in providing preparation for future leaders.

References

Armstrong, Mary Beth, J. Edward Ketz, and Dwight Owsen. 2003. "Ethics Education in Accounting: Moving Toward Ethical Motivation and Ethical Behavior." *Journal of Accounting Education* 21: 1–16.

Belay, Getinet. 1992. "Conceptual Strategies for Operationalizing Multicultural Curricula." *Journal of Education for Library and Information Science* 33: 295–306.

Chen, Christine Y., and Jonathan Hickman. 2000. "America's 50 Best Companies for Minorities." *Fortune* 142 (July): 190–200.

Colvin, Geoffrey. 1999. "The 50 Best Companies for Asians, Blacks, and Hispanics: Companies That Pursue Diversity Outperform the S&P 500. Coincidence?" *Fortune* 140 (July): 53–54.

Dean, Katie. 2000. "Study: Women Are Good for Your Biz." *Wired News* (December 6). Available: http://wired.com/news/women/0,1540,40438,00.html. (Accessed May 29, 2003).

Dilevko, Juris. 2000. "A New Approach to Teaching Research Methods Courses in LIS Program." *Journal of Education for Library and Information Science* 41: 307–29.

"Graduates Drawn to 'Ethically Sound' Companies." 2002. *Education & Training* 44: 295.

Hernon, Peter, Ronald R. Powell, and Arthur P. Young. 2002. "University Library Directors in the Association of Research Libraries: The Next Generation, Part Two." *College & Research Libraries* 63 Available: http://vnweb.hwwilsonweb.com/hww/results/results_single.jhtml?nn=11. (Accessed April 25, 2002).

Holley, Robert P. 2003. "The Ivory Tower as Preparation for the Trenches." *College & Research Libraries News* 64: 172–75.

Hutchison, Liese L. 2002. "Teaching Ethics Across the Public Relations Curriculum" *Public Relations Review* 28: 301–9.

Intagliata, J., D. Ulrich, and N. Smallwood. 2000) "Levering Leadership Competencies to Produce Leadership Brand: Creating Distinctiveness by Focusing on Strategy and Results." *Human Resource Planning* 23. Available: http://proquest.umi.com/pqdweb. (Accessed April 21, 2002).

"Is Ethics Good Business? Interview with Lynn Sharp Paine." 2003. *Challenge* 46 (March/April): 6–21.

Jasinowski, Jerry J. 2001. "Growth and the Imperative of Diversity in the Twenty-First Century." *Executive Speeches* 15: 58–61.

Jeng, Ling Hwey. 1997. "Facilitating Classroom Discussion on Diversity." *Journal of Education for Library and Information Science* 38: 334–38.

Knight, Don, Craig L. Pearce, Ken G. Smith, Judy D. Olian, et al. 1999. "Top Management Team Diversity, Group Process, and Strategic Consensus." *Strategic Management Journal* 20: 445–65.

Koonce, Richard. 2001. "Redefining Diversity: It's Not Just the Right Thing to Do. It Also Makes Good Business Sense." *Training and Development* 55: 22–33.

Kuczynski, Sherry. 1999. "If Diversity, Then Higher Profits? Companies That Have Successful Diversity Programs Seem to Have Higher Returns. But Which Came First?" *HR Magazine* 44.Available: http://www.shrm.org/hrmagazine/articles/1299div.htm. (Accessed May 29, 2002).

Lance, Keith Curry, and Julie J. Boucher. 1996. "Decision-Making by the Numbers: Available Data for Academic Library Managers." *Advances in Librarianship* 19: 1–21.

LeGris, J., and F. H. Cote. 1997. "Collaborative Partnerships in Nursing Education: A Preceptorship Model for BScN Students." *Nursing Connections* 10: 55–70.

McLaughlin, J. B. 1999. "James O. Freedman on Diversity & Dartmouth" *Change* 23: 25–31.

Moran, Barbara B. 2001. "Practitioners vs. LIS Educators: Time to Reconnect." *Library Journal* 126. Available: http://vnweb.hwwilsonweb.com/hww/shared/shared_main.jhtml;jsessionid=H52WZCQQNX2EPQA3DIKSFFY?_requestid=184744. (Accessed December 3, 2002).

Peterson, Lorna. 1994. "Teaching the Practitioners: One Professor's Attempt at Library Education and Sensitivity to Multicultural Diversity." *The Reference Librarian* 45/46: 23–38.

Peterson, Lorna. 1999. "The Definition of Diversity: Two Views: A More Specific Definition." *Journal of Library Administration* 27: 17–26.

Richards, Clinton H., Joseph Gilbert, and James R. Harris.2002. "Assessing Ethics Education Needs in the MBA Program." *Teaching Business Ethics* 6: 447.

Rudenstine, Neil. 1996. "Why a Diverse Student Body Is So Important." *Chronicle of Higher Education* 42 (April 19): B1–B2.

Sawyer, M. J., I. M. Alexander, L. Gordon, L. J. Jusczczak, and C. Gilliss. 2000. "A Critical Review of Current Nursing Faculty Practice." *Journal of the American Academy of Nurse Practitioners* 12: 511–16.

Schaeffer, Patricia. 2001. "Annual HR Salary Survey." *Training and Development* 55: 62–66.

Stevens, J. W. 1999. "Creating Collaborative Partnership: Clinical Intervention Research in an Inner-City Middle School." *Social Work in Education* 21: 151–62.

Vest, G. W., J. Ronnau, B. R. Lopez, and G. Gonzales, G. 1997. "Alternative Health Practices in Ethnically Diverse Rural Areas: A Collaborative Research Project." *Health and Social Work* 22: 95–100.

Welburn, William. 1994. "Do We Really Need Cultural Diversity in the Library and Information Science Curriculum." *Journal of Education for Library and Information Science* 35: 328–30.

Williams, James F., II, and Mark D. Winston. 2003. "Leadership Competencies and the Importance of Research Methods and Statistical Analysis in Decision Making and Research and Publication: A Study of Citation Patterns." *Library and Information Science Research* 25.

Winston, Mark D. 2001a. "Communication and Teaching: Education about Diversity in the LIS Classroom." *Journal of Library Administration* 33: 199–212.

Winston, Mark. 2001b. "The Importance of Leadership Diversity: The Relationship Between Diversity and Organizational Success in the Academic Environment." *College & Research Libraries* 62: 517–26.

Winston, Mark. 2002. "Diversity and Curricula in Undergraduate Business and MBA Programs." Unpublished manuscript, 1–15.

Winston, Mark, and Debbie Fisher. in press. "Leadership Education for Young Adult Librarians: A Research Study." *Public Library Quarterly*.

Winston, Mark, and Gretchen Hazlin. in press. "Leadership Competencies in Library and Information Science: Marketing as a Component of LIS Curricula." *Journal of Education for Library and Information Science*.

Winston, Mark, and Haipeng Li. 2000. "Managing Diversity in Liberal Arts College Libraries." *College & Research Libraries* 61: 205–15.

Ethics and Human Resource Management in Academic Libraries

William C. Welburn

Since 1999 readers of the Sunday *New York Times Magazine* have been entertained by ethical advice offered by "the Ethicist," *Times* columnist Randy Cohen. Though not a philosopher by training, Cohen counsels his readers on practical matters of everyday life, giving advice that has prompted a bevy of interest if not controversy.[1] Cohen's popular column reflects a broader social concern for the practice of ethics in all walks of life. The thirst for resolutions to ethical dilemmas faced by the public is substantial and far reaching. For example, a quick review of a fifteen-day slice of the *New York Times* found that ethical issues were focal points of twenty-five substantive articles on topics ranging from business and finance to sports, technology, and politics.[2]

The practice of ethics and ethical behavior at work is no exception to the broader discussion. According to Dorothy Foote, a Senior Lecturer in Human Resource Management at University College Northampton, "Much has been written about the role of the Human Resource Management function and its ability to respond to competitive pressures," of which a substantial amount of time and effort is devoted to reconciling the "rhetoric and reality" of ethics and managing employees in organizations of various types (Foote 2001, 25–26). Academic libraries, much like the charities that Foote studies, are likely to face an inconsistency between professional ethics and organizational values that are explicit and contextually articulated to support learning and the free and open pursuit of ideas and internal managerial practice of those same values with their own employees (Foote 2001, 36). This chapter aims to further explore ethics and human resource management by first examining recent scholarship on ethics and formal organizations, then situating those issues in the specific context of academic libraries to prompt further thinking about how academic library administrators and, in particular, human resource managers, might create an ethical work climate.

Durkheim's Dilemma

A century ago Emil Durkheim expressed concern over the role of ethics and morality in a society that is increasingly dominated by corporations. Referring to lack of organization of ethics among businesses, Durkheim wrote: "There exists to-day a whole range of collective activity outside the sphere of morals and which is almost entirely removed from the moderating effect of obligations"(1958, 9–10). John Hendry, in an insightful essay on the sociology of business ethics, argued that Durkheim held that "moral rules were socially constructed and that they would and should change as society evolved" (2001, 204). According to Hendry, Durkheim believed that there was an intermediary level between the individual and society that required moral discipline, and organizations resided at this intermediary level. Although for many years bureaucracy supplanted the need for defining a moral framework for organizations to act upon, recent developments have caused organizations to shift from a bureaucratic to a networked and market-driven character, and where egoism becomes a crucial moral perspective, organizations find themselves outside of the sphere of morals, losing the moderating effect of bureaucracy.

Hendry further states that today's economy for organizations gives free agency to employees and economic self-interest to entrepreneurial managers:

> If his [Durkheim's] analysis is correct, and market self-interest proves to be both corrosive of moral values throughout society and unable, in itself, to support a stable society, then we are faced with a very serious social problem—arguably, indeed, with the single most important problem facing our society today. (2001, 204)

Many professions are governed by recognizable and carefully crafted ethics. For instance, the Association of College and Research Libraries and its parent organization, the American Library Association, have fully articulated codes of ethics for librarians and libraries vis-à-vis services that are consistent with Durkheim's concern for moral agency among professionals. However, it is only assumed that professional ethics as articulated by professional associations are absorbed by managers in organizations. The role and function of personnel and human resources, which traditionally has been ambiguously defined in organizations, has sharpened only in recent years and in accordance with competitive pressures placed upon organizations. Carolyn Wiley has found that in the corporate sector human resource professionals have been caught in a dilemma of enacting ethics at an organizational level in the face of strategic, market-driven managerial decision making:

> HR-Related professionals are bound by an altruistic norm of service and a code of ethics that directs them to honestly represent the welfare and interests of all parties including management, employees, the community, and society. General management, however, views the interests of the organization as its foremost responsibility. (1998, 147)

Supporting Hendry's analysis of Durkheim, Wiley reported that little evidence existed to suggest that human resource managers exert much influence on the ethical practices of their organizations. Wiley reexamined data from a 1992 survey, "Ethical Issues in Human Resource Management," which identified the five most serious ethical situations facing personnel and human resources administrators:

- Hiring, training or promotion based on favoritism

- Sexual harassment

- Using discipline for managerial and nonmanagerial personnel inconsistently

- Non-performance factors used in appraisals, and

- Allowing differences in pay, discipline, and promotion, due to friendships with top management. (1998, 150)

In her own reevaluation of the survey data, Wiley found that

> Employment managers' ethical behavior is generally influenced by senior managers' and supervisors' behaviors, personal values, and internal drive to succeed. In addition, employment managers believe that ethical misconduct occurs more often in particular specialties such as employment, health, safety, and security, and compensation. The most serious problems occur in these same areas. (1998, 157)

The challenge for academic libraries and other organizations is to align strategy and the strategic positioning of the library in its organizational environment—the college or university—with an ethical work climate. Bart Victor and John Cullen defined work climate as "perceptions that 'are psychologically meaningful molar descriptions that people can agree characterize a system's practices and procedures.' . . . The prevailing perceptions of typical organizational practices and procedures that have ethical content constitute the ethical work climate" (1988, 101). An ethical work climate is manifested in implementation of the concepts of civility and integrity among employees, not only in their dealings with clientele but also with each other. The tone for an ethical work climate permeates all levels of the organization and is critical to its success. As Jeffrey Pfeffer put it, "Successful organizations understand the importance of implementation, not just strategy, and moreover, recognize the crucial role of their people in this process" (1998, 16). In other words, a work climate that is cognizant of ethical considerations as they affect its employees is also likely to be positioned to perform well in its mission. And by extension, such a library will reconcile internal personnel practices with externally focused values for service, thereby settling the Durkheimian dilemma.

Some Examples

Returning to the 1992 "Ethical Issues in Human Resource Management" survey, what are the ethical dilemmas that libraries are likely to face in the administration of personnel and human resources? The remainder of this chapter explores ethical issues in an academic library setting, as extrapolated from the five most serious ethical situations covered in that survey.

Hiring, Training, or Promotion Based on Favoritism

It is a challenge for libraries to avoid favoritism in making hiring decisions, providing training and professional development opportunities, or advancing employees through the ranks and to maintain fairness and equity. Resisting favoritism is more than acting affirmatively or living within EEOC guidelines and regulations. Resisting favoritism ensures an ethical work climate in which all employees are assured objectivity in personnel and human resource processes. Keeping favoritism in check may contradict some of a library's cherished cultural traditions. For instance, many supervisors will encourage student assistants to enroll in MLIS programs in an effort to recruit outstanding library professionals. Yet those same supervisors are confronted with difficult ethical considerations when their students apply for positions in their units. At this point the line between effective mentoring and favoritism toward individuals in competitive applicant pools becomes blurred for the supervisor who wants to hire outstanding employees yet maintain a fair and equitable hiring process.

Sexual Harassment

Academic libraries provide excellent learning environments for college students, particularly for those with little or no work experience. One of the unintended learning experiences, however, may come as a result of difficulties in the everyday work environment. Student assistants can often be transient employees and, as such, may have had no training in sexual harassment in the workplace. Supervisors are challenged to work with students who work in close proximity to one another balanced against their social relationships away from the workplace. It is inevitable that unwelcome sexual advances, jokes, and pranks are likely to be seen as forms of sexual harassment when practiced by student assistants at work in the library. Even seemingly innocuous behavior such as wearing T-shirts or exposing tattoos with demeaning messages may offend someone at work, revealing the bridge of civility between the rights of the individual and the community.

Using Discipline for Managerial and Nonmanagerial Personnel Inconsistently

Pfeffer suggested that one of the principles of a people-centered organization is to reduce differentiation between staff wherever possible, perhaps through the utilization of teams (1998, 90). In libraries, there is the potential to enact various personnel practices by status in the organizational structure: between professionals and support staff, administrators and line staff, or by position within the organization. The library is confronted with the possibility of subverting an ethical work climate not only through inconsistent rewards but also through discrepancies in discipline, the effect of which can be demoralizing to employees.

The issue of inconsistent use of discipline also affects individuals. An ethical work climate manifested in integrity in human resource decision making is violated when employees perceive differential treatment when discipline is administered to resolve a problem. Perhaps one of the best remedies is suggested by Pfeffer; when an organization invests in a team, the team rather than the individual is held responsible for the consequences of their actions.

Nonperformance Factors Used in Appraisals

Nothing causes greater frustration for a library human resource administrator than to learn that an employee's decision to leave, revealed during an exit interview, had to do with nonperformance factors used in the employee's appraisal. What recourse can be taken during an exit interview when nonperformance factors are the cause of an employee's departure? The effect on the organization—to say nothing of the individual—is growing resentment and the potential for turnover by an increasingly uncommitted workforce that may identify the appraisal process as subjective and unfair, likely leading to further erosion of an ethical work climate.

Allowing Differences in Pay, Discipline, and Promotion Due to Friendships with Top Management

Libraries, like other organizations, are challenged to balance fair processes, especially as they relate to pay increases and promotion, with wage increases for individual employees that are based on a desire to retain valued employees. Managers are challenged to mediate conflict between employees or whole units that perceive growing salary inequity. Human resource managers are directed to ensure that the processes for salary awards and promotion do not reflect the personal associations between administrators and employees.

Most organizations provide their employees with salary increases based on individual merit. Yet there are serious shortcomings in the practice of merit-based salary increases. As Pfeffer has noted, one of the problems with merit pay is that "in many instances, it is not based very much on 'merit' " (1998, 206). It is also possible that an employee who is consistently judged meritorious will reach a salary cap and will not be able to grow without promotion to a higher level in the organization. Finally, merit in this context may be linked to the status or worth of an employee's job assignments. A library may unintentionally give an advantage to an employee in a merit-based pay environment because the employee happens to be employed in an area deemed vital to the organization. Accordingly, pay differentials may emerge from more subtle circumstances than personal friendships or favoritism.

Alternatively, libraries may choose to shift emphasis from individual to team-based reward or compensation to focus energies on productivity of the organization and consequently wash out the affronts to an ethical work climate caused by the unintended consequences of favoring individual employees.

Conclusion

This chapter explored Durkheim's concern for the place of morality and ethics in organizations as they occupy an important space between the individual and society. As Heidi von Weltzien Hoivik suggested, there is a need to look more closely at "the ambivalent relationship between a person's professional ethical values as collectively held values and those expected to be adhered to on the organizational level" (2002, 3). She concluded:

> If we are serious about business and professional ethics, we must pay more attention to the emerging knowledge-based network organizations where personal and professional accountability re-emerge with renewed importance. We need to increase managerial awareness as to why and how it is not only possible but necessary to leverage professional ethics effectively. (2002, 10)

The human resources administrator in libraries is often called on to straddle two roles, that of a strategist and that of the conscience of the organization. In academic libraries, human resources administrators are at their best when they assume the role of strategist and, conversely, are weakest when they function as the moral conscience of every personnel decision. By working to create strategies to improve the ethical work climate in academic libraries with common-sense concerns for civility and integrity, libraries and their human resources managers are likely to achieve organizational success and the Durkheimian ideal of an organizational moral conscience.

Notes

1. For a discussion of the negative responses Cohen has received about his column, see Cohen (2002).

2. Articles published between April 1 and April 15, 2003 at www. nytimes.com.

References

Cohen, Randy. 2002. "The Politics of Ethics." *The Nation* (April 8). Available: http://www.thenation.com/doc.mhtml?i=20020408&s=cohen. (Accessed April 18, 2003).

Durkheim, Emile. 1958. *Professional Ethics and Civic Morals.* Translated by Cornelia Brookfield. Glencoe, IL: Free Press.

Foote, Dorothy. 2001. "The Question of Ethical Hypocrisy in Human Resource Management in the U.K. and Irish Charity Sectors." *Journal of Business Ethics* 34: 25–38.

Foote, Dorothy, and Izabela Robinson. 1999. "The Role of the Human Resources Manager: Strategist or Conscience of the Organisation?" *Business Ethics: A European Review* 8 (April): 88–98.

Hendry, John. 2001. "After Durkheim: An Agenda for the Sociology of Business Ethics." *Journal of Business Ethics* 34: 209–18.

Hoivik, Heidi von Weltzien. 2002. "Professional Ethics—a Managerial Opportunity in Emerging Organizations." *Journal of Business Ethics* 39: 3–11.

Pfeffer, Jeffrey. 1998. *The Human Equation: Building Profits by Putting People First.* Boston: Harvard Business School Press.

Victor, Bart, and John B. Cullen. 1988. "The Organizational Bases of Ethical Work Climates." *Administrative Science Quarterly* 33: 101–25.

Wiley, Carolyn. 1998. "Reexamining Perceived Ethics Issues and Ethics Roles among Employment Managers." *Journal of Business Ethics* 17: 147–61.

Conversations with Our Leaders

Throughout the development of this book, the editors had the distinct pleasure of engaging in many interesting and thoughtful discussions with the chapter contributors on human resources issues in academic libraries. These discussions sparked ideas for other contributions, helped the editors to refine the book, and led to additional topical chapters. An interesting by-product of the discussions was the formation of an informal roster of library leaders who have helped to advance human resources issues over the years. As a follow-up on some of the ideas that surfaced during the evolution of this volume, the editors decided to talk with some of these leaders on a selected list of human resources issues.

In a review of the last three years of *Library Administration & Management*, we found articles written on an array of topics such as "Changing the Culture of Libraries," "Valuing Employees through Recognition," "Library Staff Development and Training for Assessing Services," "Fostering Collaborative Learning and Group Work in Libraries," "Assessing the Diversity Climate," and "Understanding Organizational Culture." These articles provide an examination of issues that academic library managers are grappling with, and we decided that it would be valuable for readers to get the perspectives of several library leaders on issues and trends they thought were pertinent to human resources. We also felt this would provide human resources practitioners with a glimpse of how the key issues of their field are viewed by academic library administrators. What follows is a succession of interviews with just a few of the leaders who have helped to advance human resources in academic libraries.

Leaders in the profession who agreed to be interviewed were Paul Anderson, Assistant Director for Library Administrative Services, University of Delaware Library; Nancy Baker, University Librarian, University of Iowa; Stella Bentley, Dean of Libraries, University of Kansas; Barbara Dewey, Dean of Libraries, University of Tennessee; Joan Giesecke, Dean of Libraries, University of Nebraska-Lincoln; Lance Query, Dean of Libraries & Academic Information Resources, Tulane University; and Carla Stoffle, Dean of Libraries, University of Arizona.

1.   **Looking back over the last ten years, can you identify and discuss several key human resource issues that were critical at that time and how they relate to or differ from current issues and challenges?**

PA: One of the biggest concerns in HR was training and preparing staff for change. These are still important issues that need to be kept in mind when planning for the implementation of new systems or considering how to structure and plan meaningful training opportunities. I think some consultants may have underestimated staff interest in training and development and their ability to deal with change. I sense staff are thriving in what is a very dynamic and exciting time for library and information workers. The lesson to be learned is that managers need to work harder at challenging staff. Setting expectations of excellence is the single best management strategy.

Certainly issues of equality and understanding still have a critical part in our national debate. I think HR training ten to fifteen years ago focused on understanding and acceptance of differences. Today we focus on celebrating diversity. I have seen a positive change in how diversity programs are perceived and embraced. I think the idea that diversity is one of our greatest strengths is now a strongly held view of many organizations and their staff.

The last ten to fifteen years saw the introduction of important laws which provided much needed protections for individuals and held organizations accountable for ensuring these protections. HR work involved introducing, training, and overseeing organizational implementation of ADA guidelines, FMLA policies, and the establishment of a work environment free of sexual harassment. All of these are still an important focus of HR work. The concepts are better understood and accepted now throughout organizations. The HR manager still has an important role in monitoring an organization's policies, practices, and environment.

Changes in the nature of recruitment is one of the more remarkable changes in the last decade with changes in economic health and the aging of our profession. Ten years ago we all were sifting through large pools to find the best candidate. Now we are faced with small pools and the wider concern of trying not just to fill a position, but to find ways to encourage entrance into our great profession. Good recruiters have always tried to make applicants feel welcome and shown appreciation for their willingness to visit campus and interview. We have tried to answer questions and present the candidates with a great deal of information so that they are in a position to make the best choice for themselves. Well-informed job acceptances result in good retention and a content workforce. These things which were always important to successful recruitment and retention are now essential.

The most important new issue relates to the fact that we are all increasingly connected in an increasingly virtual world. Nearly every library staff member regularly uses a microcomputer and most have them on their desks. E-mail which was seen as a potentially convenient messaging system not that many years ago is now the system for communicating about work. We all do much of our work on e-mail. The availability of e-mail and the Web have opened up the very real issue of working virtually. Constantly being connected via cell phones, wireless Web connections, work stations at home, and laptops on the road brings to a new level the issue of striking a balance in our work and personal lives.

NB: The aging workforce in libraries is a key human resources issue that comes immediately to mind. We have all read Stanley Wilder's 1995 study of the demographics of staff in ARL libraries. While we might have noticed that the staff in our own institutions were predominantly from the Baby Boomer generation or earlier, most of us did not realize that this demographic profile characterized *all* our libraries nor had we thought much about the full implications of this. Many of our older employees who have been healthy most of their adult life are now having medical problems resulting in short- or long-term absences. Many are now dealing with various issues related to care for aging, dependent parents resulting in additional absences, stress, and, in some cases, new financial responsibilities. I have heard many of our older staff express concern that they cannot afford to retire when they had first anticipated. Some of this concern stems from the current economic downfall and its impact on invested retirement funds. That may correct itself in time. But there is also concern that given the number of Baby Boomers in the U.S., Social Security may not even be available when this group retires or that it might not be worth much even if it is still around. Similarly, as the cost of health care benefits rise each year, many institutions have had to reduce the amount of coverage paid by the employer, leaving more of these costs to the individual. There is concern that, at the very time when these employees are most likely to need this coverage, they will have to work longer to afford it. Whenever you have employees who must continue to work beyond the time in which they really want to be working, there is a greater potential for less productivity, enthusiasm, and creativity. Without turnover, there will be fewer opportunities to hire new people and infuse "new blood" into the organization which is so important if an organization is to move ahead and thrive.

The other issue that comes to mind is diversity of our workforce. Over the last ten years, there has been an obvious shift in attitude, not on the part of our universities who, I believe, are still genuinely committed to diversity. But there has been a shift in attitude from the general public. People want to believe that once we have taken small steps and seen some positive results, we have actually made major gains and have done enough. Certainly, there has been real progress in the last decade developing a more diverse workforce in libraries and fostering awareness/sensitivity to difference that has made all of us more effective serving a diverse clientele. But we certainly have not done enough [and] we may see increased challenges to our diversity efforts in the future.

SB: Ten years ago we were just beginning to change our expectations for what responsibilities required an MLS and what could be handled well by skilled individuals without an MLS. We now have a number of professional positions that require specific academic training but not necessarily an MLS, and major units headed by non-MLS managers. Continuing staff development has become much more important as we have coped with both a constantly changing environment and fewer positions in our libraries. Where state or institutional rules have allowed, some of us have been able to create career ladders for the support staff, so that they can be promoted and rewarded for acquiring new skills and taking on more responsibility.

We had large pools for professional vacancies at any level ten years ago; with our salaries having lost ground in comparison with other professions, we no longer have large pools for even entry-level positions. We are more often bidding against other libraries to hire good candidates, and the salary compression that results from such a process is becoming a major problem in many libraries. I think it will be increasingly difficult to attract individuals to librarianship if our salaries do not become more competitive in the marketplace.

BD: Recruitment of qualified professional librarians and IT staff [remains the same if not more critical]; movement of librarians from production activities to higher level teaching, learning, and management activities [is not as much of an issue now]; excellent management skills and ability to plan strategically [are still an issue]; well planned and continuous training and staff development [is still an issue]; problems with campus HR services [is still an issue]; communication between levels of staff [is still an issue]; excellence in customer service in all regards [is still an issue].

JG: Issues from ten years ago include creating teams and how developing a team approach differs from other organizational approaches. From an HR viewpoint, teamwork includes skills and values that were not necessarily emphasized in organizations. Interpersonal skills, coaching, negotiation skills as well as values of group work became more important. Also, diversity was not as inclusive a term as now, and libraries were mostly at the compliance level when working on diversity issues. Today, we have moved to thinking about inclusiveness and how to incorporate everyone into the organization.

LQ: I tend to see more continuity than change on the salient HR issues that have emerged over the past decade. Most generally and importantly, the issue then and now is the quality of individuals entering our profession. What has changed is the balance between supply and demand: it's now much more of a seller's market. That said, I'm not convinced that we (the buyers) are getting a better product than a decade ago. Important among them is our profession's relative lack of professional standards for graduates (as opposed to library and IS graduate schools) vis-B-vis our professional competition. Another is our difficulty in attracting the best and brightest . . . however one wants to define that. Particularly acute is our need to get graduates with highest intellects, strongest motivation, best communication skills, etc., not to mention in-demand academic backgrounds like sciences and math. This is not limited to us as we see similar problems in primary and secondary education. A huge part of the problem for us (and them) obviously is salaries. The other part is quality control of who enters our graduate programs and our profession; of course, this, too, is directly related to salaries. That said, are our standards of entry high enough? After twenty-five + years of reviewing candidates, I have serious doubts. What's more, I don't see any appreciable improvement in the pools; they certainly are smaller. I am encouraged by the offerings and results of quality staff development programs that have emerged over the past decade all over the profession (CLIR, ARL, EDUCAUSE, ACRL, regional consortia, etc.).

    I am encouraged by the progress over the past ten years in the area of minority advancement in academic librarianship. [See below under item 6.] While not enough, I think the ARL data indicate progress, though the constraints which the profession as a whole faces (see above) continue to slow us. The fact that recently we now have more women than men as directors of ARL institutions is evidence of progress.

    Ten years (and more) ago, there was greater concern about the command of technology among us. Today, more than ever, I think the trend is toward "It's the content, stupid." That's progress and reflects, I think, the quality of preparation of our entry as well as veteran librarians via graduate work and staff development programs, respectively. As compared to ten years ago, we are both less fearful and less enamored by technology. To compare our profession to teachers yet again, the growing recognition that our teachers need to master their subject as the sine qua non of quality education rather than emphasis upon the technique of teaching is a healthy and hopeful sign.

That said, as delivery systems of higher education have become more diverse over the past decade +, so has the need for our teachers and librarians to understand how (and how differently) individuals learn. I'm encouraged by the efforts of professional organizations, literature, etc. in grappling with all of that. Much more so than a decade ago.

One human resource issue that I don't regard as key (many did, as I recall) is the faculty status issue for librarians. I'm not going into the pros and cons of that old chestnut. Suffice to say that it's a good sign that an era of "benign neglect" (to use that term as Moynihan had intended) has set in.

A key issue that was a problem a decade ago and, in my opinion, looms at least as large now is the issue of succession in our profession. Specifically, succession in the administration of academic research libraries. The past decade has seen a number of developments that have challenged our ability to ensure quality administrators. They include: The flattening of our organizations; I believe this to be generally a positive move, especially in light of budget cuts or only modest increases and in encouraging quality ideas to reach to the top. However, this has been accompanied by career plateauing and, in many institutions, the "disruption" of a "natural progression" of early and mid-career potential quality administrators. In extreme cases, the simple reduction of staff has had the same effect.

CS: Issues include Diversity (recruitment and retention), Salaries, Staff Development/staff learning opportunities, Gearing up to operate in teams (for us), Growing leadership skills in all staff, Mentoring junior librarians, Empowering staff and growing their roles in the organization, and Changing positions and new positions with new skills. These are all still issues today. We haven't as a profession really done much too seriously address these. We mostly say they are out of our control or that when we get more money we will do something.

2.   What human resource expectations do you now have of managers in your organization?

PA: I am not sure this has changed except that the values of what I would call enlightened management seem now to be held in common by most people assuming management positions.

I would define enlightened management as management that expresses interest in the well-being of employees, their development, and their ideas. It is an approach that recognizes the manager's role in developing human resources in addition to managing a particular operation. Implicit in this is a willingness to work with staff to improve performance. Enlightened management means more success in recruitment, retention, evaluation, organization and directly relates to the success of work groups.

I expect managers to be conversant with good HR practices and be knowledgeable concerning the policies and procedures of the organization. Finally, I encourage managers to be positive in their approach to solving problems and especially to supervising staff.

Respect for individuals regardless of gender, sexual orientation, ethnicity, religion, political ideas, affiliations, or handicaps is a vital expectation for all staff. A related value that I encourage is the celebration of diversity. Respect for diversity is the minimum, but the goal is celebrating diversity.

NB: I expect managers *to manage* their departments in good times and in bad. They need to be leaders within their own departments and within the libraries as a whole. I expect them to represent the interests of their department and consider the greater needs of the libraries and university as we set policy and directions as our organization. This global view is what they need to foster in their staff as well. Managers need to work with their staff to establish well chosen priorities for each year that are consistent with the strategic directions of the Libraries and the University. They must coach and mentor each member of the department to develop his/her talents and grow as individuals and as professionals. Staff need regular feedback on their performance and I expect managers to do that. I am especially insistent that they conduct performance evaluations on schedule. They need to keep their supervisor informed of major developments and problems in a timely manner. Finally, I expect them to handle problems when they occur and not wait until they become catastrophes. Many organizations suffer from "good time" managers who want to do the fun parts of the job and ignore or mishandle personnel performance problems and other less fun challenges. Their successors and/or administrators end up cleaning up messes that would have been much less problematic had they only been addressed effectively when they first occurred.

SB: Managers today are expected to communicate well with their employees, continually seek opportunities to streamline and improve operations, be more user-centered in their thinking, and lead change. They are also expected to be able to work well in a much more team-centered environment both within their unit and across all units than most libraries had ten years ago.

BD: That they take seriously the need to mentor, train, and develop their staff; that they constantly review staffing needs and adjust accordingly; that they delegate as much as possible making full use of staff talent and expertise; that they use the notion of shared governance in their interaction with staff—i.e., have regular staff meetings, etc.

JG: Managers need to think in terms of coaching and facilitating rather than command and control. Managers need to build an environment that is inclusive. Listening skills are crucial. Also, managers are not the "parents" of a unit and can no longer treat employees as "children" who can be told what to do.

LQ: I'll combine responses to questions 2 and 3: Clearly, managers need to know how scholarly information is created, disseminated, and preserved. Similarly, they need to know how our users acquire and use that information. That sounds so simple and obvious, but I think we lose sight of that as we look for "managerial" skills. They need to understand how our various kinds of libraries (school, special, public, and academic research) fit into the information delivery systems. They need to know the product before they can manage its creation, dissemination, preservation, etc. They need to know something (a lot?) about human behavior, motivation, etc. Communication skills are critical, starting with the ability to listen . . . to both staff and user. More than ever, managers need to be entrepreneurs as the expectations for our libraries exceed any reasonable expectation of requisite resources. Business-like approaches should be understood, if not always embraced: the potential and techniques of strategic planning; R&D, marketing, evaluation/analysis, accounting and accountability, etc. Sometimes managers have a "leave it to administration" to deliver the resources, set the priorities, etc. attitude; their skill set should include an ownership ethos. Associated with that, skill in coalition building both within and outside of the university setting is critical and communication skills are a critical requisite.

Too seldom do our graduate programs emphasize ethics . . . though that is changing, especially in graduate business education. Too seldom do we emphasize ethics with our managers and staff; perhaps because we take it for granted that, given our calling, we are ethical. Risky assumption. Our managers face ethical dilemmas all the time, yet we aren't preparing them for that. Over the past decade there has been increased recognition for the need of quality mentoring, but it seems to me that recognition of that need has exceeded delivery. Besides, mentoring itself cannot counteract the effects of practical career-progressional experience that was mentioned above.

Just as education and research has become more multi- and cross-disciplinary, so have information delivery systems. Associated with that phenomenon and in light of financial challenges, our managers need to develop effective teams. Teamwork is broadly recognized as important, but are our managers skilled in implementing that need? Again, I think we take that for granted, perhaps because we assume good intentions and noble goals.

CS: We have developed a set of expectations (13) for team leaders that further the Library's mission. Some of these include:

- Works proactively and constructively to identify, define, and solve problems with own team and between teams and other individuals and teams. Works with team members to develop coaching mechanism to having performance problems.

- Facilitates and involves all team members in team planning, objectives setting, and problem solving, empowering and holding team members accountable for participation and results.

- Works with teams to define team and team leaders roles and appropriate methodology for decision-making. Seeks and utilizes data and objective criteria for decision-making. Helps team recognize options and consequences of team decisions. Has final accountability for seeing that decisions get made and that there is appropriate follow through.

- Communicates and leads development of team understanding and support of librarywide decisions and priorities; helps the team communicate and create understanding of team issues librarywide.

- Helps promote and support diversity within the team and the Library.

- Leads in management of budgets and fosters understanding of and responses to internal and external funding opportunities and constraints.

3. Is there a critical skill set that they need?

PA: Today's managers must be effective at working in and with groups. You need lots of people in an organization that have this ability. Even the most specialized technical skills are secondary in importance. What is needed far more than just interpersonal effectiveness is effectiveness with groups. A manager's willingness to share information and practice good communication is critical. Most differences of opinion which result in disaffection are the result of poor communication. Managers must communicate effectively and willingly to be successful. Managers must be open to new ideas and new ways to solve problems. Effective managers understand the importance of how to do something. Attention to effective process is the key to good and lasting solutions. Managers today must be also be open to working with and applying technology.

NB: Absolutely. They need to know how to work effectively as a group facilitator, how to manage conflict productively, and how to work with people who have different learning styles and ways of doing things so these differences become assets not liabilities for the department. Managers also need to be familiar with basic personnel policies of the institution and procedures that have been established to deal with serious problems.

Clearly the Libraries' and University's Human Resources professionals will be a resource for dealing with the latter, but it is important for managers to have some basic knowledge to handle the most common situations. Training on how to manage time and juggle a variety of responsibilities is also important. Managers often do not have full control of their agenda for the day – unexpected things must take precedence over what they may have planned. It is essential to know how to manage this all-too-common situation. These are all skills that can be developed through training and experience.

SB: They have to be able to look critically at the operations of their unit and be very good at personnel management. As our parent institutions expect more accountability from the library, the library administration is expecting much more accountability from middle managers.

BD: Excellent management skills; leadership skills; excellent written and oral communication skills; excellent listening skills; ability to motivate and inspire.

JG: Negotiating, coaching, listening, good communication skills. Be facilitators.

LQ: Response combined with item 2.

4.   Aside from managers, how do you view the role of human resources professionals in your organization?

PA: A really important role that fosters long-term organizational well-being is advocacy for staff development programs. A related role is to serve as facilitator of organizational development and effectiveness. The HR professional should be a knowledgeable advocate on best practices related to HR. Listening is a key function. The HR professional is sometimes in a position to listen to concerns and advise or refer staff and managers and thereby assist in solving problems.

NB: I think they have three major roles. First of all, they are the individuals who ensure that the Libraries are operating in compliance with university policies and procedures with respect to human resource issues and that library managers are applying campus human resources policies and procedures appropriately, consistently, and equitably in the Libraries. Second, the human resource professionals are a critical consultant for library managers and staff on how best to handle the wide range of human resources situations and problems they face over the course of their tenure with the institution. Finally, they are the individuals who can best influence the university's human resources policies and procedures to reflect the needs of the Libraries. They are generally the individuals who serve on campus human resources committees and task forces, who review drafts of policies and procedures, and who bring special problems or needs of library staff and managers to the attention of the campus human resources professionals. These are all important roles.

SB: Given the number of personnel in large academic libraries, the HR professional in the library is crucial to the smooth functioning of many activities. The most important areas are:

- providing advice and counseling supervisors and employees on a range of issues;
- overseeing the recruitment and hiring process;
- overseeing a staff development/continuing education program;
- overseeing the evaluation process(es);
- liaison to the parent institution's HR department.

BD: Of critical importance to the organization.

JG: HR professionals provide leadership, keeping up with the changes and issues in HR management and helping the organization address these changes. Also, I expect HR professionals to keep up with changing legal issues and help managers work with these changes. For example, implementing Family Medical Leave policies requires training managers and staff to understand how the law works, as well as how local procedures are to be implemented.

LQ: HR managers' role is both defensive and offensive. Defensive because it's their expertise that helps keep the library organization and administration out of trouble, (e.g., bad behavior like breaking the law, etc.) That's obvious and I won't elaborate here. The other is the role of partner in making the library "be all that it can be," specifically, through the value-added expertise they can bring to our administrators and managers. They enable us to avoid reinventing the wheel by knowing the issues, facts, theories, best practices, etc., in their areas such as team-building, law, motivation theory and practice, training programs and techniques, planning techniques, recruitment, rewards, performance evaluation, and, increasingly, conflict resolution. The list goes on and on. Library administrators and managers generally rely upon what has worked for them in specific instances. Not a bad practice, but perhaps shortsighted. I have appreciated HR professionals at their best when they are not only resources and consultants, but also gadflies and sort of ministers without portfolio; those roles can be tricky and often off-putting, but valuable to all in the library when well done.

CS: They need to grow and change just as we expect staff to do. They need to be part not set apart from the organization. They need to find ways to help the organization achieve its goals.

5.   **Over the years, are there any human resources initiatives that you were directly involved in that you were particularly proud of? What are they, and why do they stand out for you?**

PA: I have been an advocate of staff assistance programs most of my professional career.

I have been very active in the Library's diversity program. I have particularly enjoyed being the administrative liaison with the Library Diversity Committee. We have developed many fine programs for the Library and I have enjoyed working with the Committee.

The Pauline A. Young Residency is a wonderful post-master's residency program here at the University of Delaware. Although I am not the person most responsible for the program, I do work closely with the Library departments about projects for the Residency and also work with the resident.

I always have been proud of our recruiting and staffing function. I am always pleased when someone who did not get offered a job says that they enjoyed the interview experience at the University of Delaware. We want people to leave interviews with a high regard for the institution and an interest in interviewing with the organization again.

NB: Certainly, I am most proud of the two diversity initiatives undertaken by the Association of Research Libraries (ARL) while I was chair of the Association's Diversity Committee. The ARL Leadership and Career Development Program have offered outstanding leadership skills development for mid-career librarians from underrepresented groups. ARL directors have an opportunity to mentor these librarians during this program. As of 2003, the program has "graduated" three classes of participants and it has been wonderful to see so many of these talented librarians move into management positions within university libraries so quickly after they completed the program. The second initiative established scholarships for librarians from underrepresented groups to earn their MLS degree and work in university libraries. This initiative was designed to create a better pipeline of librarians from diverse backgrounds into university libraries. Together these two initiatives were concrete activities that have been sustained and improved over the years by ARL. While credit for these initiatives lies with many ARL library directors and the ARL staff, I am proud that the committee I chaired accomplished tangible and beneficial activities to foster diversity in research libraries. I am especially proud of these initiatives because, too frequently, we pay lip service to the benefits and importance of diversity without really doing anything to make our organizations more diverse.

I have also been proud of my efforts to bring more of our non-librarian staff into the decision-making process in libraries. Our libraries are fortunate to have many talented, highly educated individuals in our non-librarian positions. We need the ideas, talents, and experience of all our staff to move our organizations forward. I have tried to appoint more of them to committees and other decision-making entities in the Libraries at two universities.

SB: I am especially proud of two initiatives that became operational while I was Dean of Libraries at Auburn University: reestablishing a minority residency program for individuals who had just acquired the MLS and creating a career ladder program for classified staff.

BD: There are many including at Iowa: implementation of diversity committee and the minority residency program; inclusion of strategic planning, excellent recruitment record; good progress on staff development and training; mentoring librarians to present and publish; at Tennessee implementation of our award winning diversity committee, diversity definition, minority residency program, extensive travel support and professional development support, great faculty productivity on research and presentations; excellent technology training series; inclusive faculty retreats.

JG: The Libraries developed a set of core competencies for all staff positions and for library faculty positions. The process of developing competencies involved a library committee working with the administration to develop and have accepted the competencies. The library faculty reviewed the core competencies and adopted the principles involved as part of a revision of the standards for promotion and tenure. The University of Nebraska used the Libraries' core competencies as a starting point for developing a set of competencies that apply to all job families across the campus system. The competencies outline the knowledge, skills, abilities, and aptitudes we need from our staff to cope with a changing environment and succeed in the twenty-first century.

LQ: The HR initiatives that I have been involved with that I am particularly proud of are the ones in which I was able to observe first-hand meaningful changes in the area of performance improvement of staff and/or the library and in the professional lives of the participants. In no particular order:

Co-author of "Shaping the Future: The Association of Southeastern Research Libraries' Competencies for Research Librarians."

Member of Conflict Management System Design Task Force at Tulane. University-wide initiative the goal of which is described in title.

Reform of goal setting and performance appraisal system University-wide at Tulane in which my complaining of status quo and offering the Library as model and test-site has resulted in superior goal-setting and performance evaluation system. Widely applauded by staff throughout the organization.

Creation of staff organization at Library at Tulane to be advocate for paraprofessionals; previously basically a social function group. Now eyes and ears and mouth of staff.

Successfully strong advocate for merit salary and wage adjustments in a tense environment of union-management conflict. Was representative of deans in contract negotiation between AAUP and Administration in campus-wide contract at Western Michigan University.

Successfully emphasized meritocracy in salary and wage systems at three universities in various capacities as Personnel Librarian, Assistant University Librarian, and Dean.

Principal in development of information literacy outreach between Tulane librarians and teachers in the New Orleans Public Schools.

Co-developed and implemented cooperative CLIR-sponsored professional development program for librarians at Northwestern University, University of Chicago, and University of Illinois-Chicago.

CS: I believe we have empowered staff and helped them grow into meaningful work and we have reallocated money to pay them as close to market as possible.

6.   Over the last decade we have devoted much attention to diversity. Given the continued attacks on affirmative action, should we change our tactics and approaches to diversity? If so, why?

PA: If the courts rule against affirmative action, which I sincerely hope they do not, we will have to adjust our strategy. I think someone has said that adjustment is not retreat. I think adjustments can be made that will allow us to still address equity and fairness issues and promote diversity in the workplace. I think any setback will be temporary. It has to be because the emerging world economy and growth in worldwide communication and connectiveness is going to favor organizations that realize the goals and benefits of diversity.

NB: Since our diversity efforts largely focus on recruitment and retention of personnel from diverse backgrounds and on ways to make our libraries more welcoming to all, I doubt seriously that most of our efforts will need to change dramatically regardless of recent challenges to affirmative action. When we recruit for a position, once we sort out the candidates who meet required qualifications, there are many other factors that are considered when making a final choice. Evaluating each candidate, beyond the required qualifications, can often be rather subjective, which is why different members of a search committee are likely to evaluate each candidate differently. I believe that affirmative action means that we make diversity an important factor, but not the only factor to be considered. I have never seen anyone hired under the umbrella of affirmative action that does not meet required qualifications and emerge as a candidate of choice when the full package of skills, talents, and experiences are reviewed.

However, those of us who have minority residency programs, where positions are specifically earmarked for entry-level librarians from underrepresented groups, may be forced to change these programs as a result of legal challenges to affirmative action. But these programs do not and should not represent our total efforts to diversify our workforce. If we have to abandon them, we need to find another strategy that will permit us to hire a workforce that brings the widest range of talents, perspectives, and experiences to our libraries so we can best serve our increasingly diverse clientele.

SB: I don't think so. The reasons that we have worked to increase diversity among our employees and to create a welcoming and nourishing environment for all people who use or work in our libraries are still valid.

BD: No, we need to continue to approach diversity in a comprehensive way and keep working toward a welcoming environment for a diverse population and staffed by a diverse population.

JG: Diversity is very important to our organizations. We have moved to a definition of diversity that emphasizes inclusiveness, and that looks at all the ways we are the same and the ways we differ from each other. We have moved from simply looking at compliance with the law, to developing and implementing training programs to help everyone work more effectively together to meet the goals of the organization. We need to be sure we are hiring as diverse a staff as we can, are trying to meet the needs of all of our patrons, and are thinking about how best to customize our services to meet different needs.

LQ: The attacks on affirmative action will continue whether we change our tactics or not. Will changing our tactics enhance diversity in our profession? Hard to say since neither the question nor leaders in the profession have, to my knowledge, come up with convincing alternatives to our current efforts, which I regard as fairly effective. I think this is a "bottle-half-full or half-empty" situation. Seems to me our "tactics" of affirmative action have been successful if statistical indicators are to be believed. The amicus briefs recently filed by corporate and military leaders before the Supreme Court in the University of Michigan case also witness success. Absent judicial rulings to the contrary, I think a steady-as-she-goes approach is prudent. In the context of our profession, I think remuneration will speak volumes in enhancing diversity.

CS: We must be steadfast in diversifying our organizations and creating climates that promote and welcome diversity. We must embrace diversity as a minimum qualification and hire all new staff with an understanding of what it means to work in a diverse organization. We must educate existing staff as to how to recruit effectively, implementing our diversity value in every hire not just "affirmative action hires."

Conclusion

As this conversation with library leaders indicates, much has changed over the years in human resources, and much is yet to be accomplished. Issues that continue to grow in importance include recruitment, retention, need for changing management styles, diversity, leadership, and mentoring. Through forward-looking leadership, administrators and human resources professionals working together will continue to find ways to meet the changing staffing needs in academic libraries.

The Editors

Selected Readings

Abbott, Andrew. "Professionalism and the Future of Librarianship." *Library Trends* 46 (Winter 1999): 430–43.

Ad Hoc Task Force on Recruitment & Retention Issues, a Subcommittee of the Personnel Administrators and Staff Development Officers Discussion Group. *Recruitment, Retention, and Restructuring: Human Resources in Academic Libraries*. Chicago: Association of College & Research Libraries, 2002.

ARL Research Library and Management Committee. *Library Staff Development Programs: Key Components*. Washington, DC: Association of Research Libraries, January 2003. Available: http://www.arl.org/olms/staffdev/key_components.html.

Avery, Elizabeth F., Terry Dahlin, and Deborah A. Carver, eds. *Staff Development: A Practical Guide*. 3d ed. Chicago: American Library Association, 2001.

Baldwin, David A. *The Academic Librarians Human Resources Handbook*. Englewood, CO: Libraries Unlimited, 1996.

Beck, M. A. "Technology Competencies in the Continuous Quality Improvement Environment, a Framework for Appraising the Performance of Library Public Services Staff." *Library Administration & Management* 16 (Spring 2002): 69–72.

Bennis, Warren, and Burt Nanus. *Leaders: Strategies for Taking Charge*. New York: HarperCollins, 1997.

Bolman, Lee G., and Terrence E. Deal. *Reframing Organizations: Artistry, Choice, and Leadership*. 2d ed. San Francisco: Jossey-Bass, 1997.

Bousseau, Don, and Susan K. Martin. "The Accidental Profession: Seeking the Best and the Brightest." *Journal of Academic Librarianship* 21 (May 1995) 198–99.

Brewer, Julie. "Post-master's Residency Programs: Enhancing the Development of New Professionals and Minority Recruitment in Academic and Research Libraries." *College & Research Libraries* 58 (November 1997): 528–37.

Cogell, Raquel V., and Cindy A. Gruwell, eds. *Diversity in Libraries: Academic Residency Programs*. Westport, CT: Greenwood Press, 2001.

Cox, Taylor. *Creating the Multicultural Organization: A Strategy for Capturing the Power of Diversity*. San Francisco: Jossey-Bass, 2001.

Creth, Sheila D. "Optimizing Organization Design for the Future." *Educause Quarterly* 23 (April 2000): 32–38.

Creth, Sheila D., and Frederick Duda, eds. *Personnel Administration in Libraries*. New York: Neal-Schumann, 1989.

Ely, Robin J., and David. A. Thomas. "Cultural Diversity at Work: The Effects of Diversity Perspectives on Work Group Processes and Outcomes." *Administrative Science Quarterly* 46 (2001): 229–73.

Employee Assistance Professional Association. *EAPA Standards and Professional Guidelines for Employee Assistance Programs*. Arlington, VA: EAPA, 1998.

Foote, Dorothy. "The Question of Ethical Hypocrisy in Human Resources Management in the U.K. and the Irish Charity Sector." *Journal of Business Ethics* 34 (2001): 25–26.

Gallinsky, Ellen, and James T. Bond. *The Business Work-Life Study, 1998: A Sourcebook*. New York: Families and Work Institute, 1998.

Garcha, R., and J. Phillips. "U.S. Academic Librarians: Their Involvement in Union Activities." *Library Review* 50 (2001):122–27.

Giesecke, Joan, ed. *Practical Help for New Supervisors*. 3d ed. Chicago: American Library Association, 1997.

Giesecke, Joan, and Beth McNeil. "Core Competencies and the Learning Organization." *Library Administration & Management* 13 (Summer 1999): 158–66.

Holloway, Karen. "Developing Core and Mastery-Level Competencies for Librarians." *Library Administration & Management* 17 (Spring 2003): 94–98.

Hovekamp, Tina. M. "Organizational Commitment of Professional Employees in Union and Nonunion Research Libraries." *College & Research Libraries* 55 (July 1994):297–307.

———. "Unionization and Job Satisfaction Among Professional Library Employees in Academic Research Institutions." *College & Research Libraries* 55 (July 1994): 341–50.

Hurt, Tara L., and Sunday, Deborah S. "Career Paths for Paraprofessionals: Your Ladder to Success." *Library Administration & Management* 16 (Fall 2002): 198–202.

Jurow, Susan. "Core Competencies: Strategic Thinking about the Work We Choose to Do." *The Journal of Academic Librarianship* 22 (July 1996): 300–2.

Kaufman, Paula T. *Where Do the Next "We" Come From? Recruiting, Retaining, and Developing Our Successors.* ARL Bimonthly Report 221. Washington, DC: Association of Research Libraries, 2002.

Kearns, Paul. *Measuring and Managing Employee Performance: A Practical Manual to Maximize Organizational Performance Through People.* London: Pearsal Education Limited, 2000.

Kight, Dawn V., and Carolyn Snyder. "Library Staff Development and Training for Assessment of Services." *Library Administration & Management* 16 (Winter 2002): 24–27.

Kroll, Rebecca. "Beyond Evaluation: Performance Appraisal as a Planning and Motivational Tool in Libraries." *The Journal of Academic Librarianship* 9 (1983): 27–32.

Line, Maurice B., and Margaret Kinnell. "Human Resource Management in Library and Information Services." *Annual Review of Information Science and Technology* 28 (1993): 317–59.

Lynch, Beverly P., and Kimberley Robes Smith, "The Changing Nature of Work in Academic Libraries." *College and Research Libraries* 62 (September 2001): 407–20.

Mayo, Diane, and Jeanne Goodrich. *Staffing for Results: A Guide to Working Smarter.* Chicago: American Library Association, 2002.

McCook, Kathleen de la Pena. "Human Resources Management: Ethics in Personnel." *Ethics and the Librarian,* 101–13. Edited by F. W. Lancaster. Urbana, IL: University of Illinois at Urbana-Champaign, Graduate School of Library and Information Science, 1991.

McNamara, Carter. "Managing Ethics in the Workplace." *Journal of Information Ethics* 8 (Fall 1999): 5–8.

Mech, Terrence F., and Gerard B. McCabe, eds. *Leadership and Academic Librarians.* Westport, CT.: Greenwood Press. 1998.

Musser, Linda R. "What We Say and What We Reward: Valuing Employees Through Recognition Programs." *Library Administration & Management* 15 (2001): 85–89.

O'Reilly, Charles A., III, and Jeffrey Pfeffer. *Hidden Value: How Great Companies Achieve Extraordinary Results with Ordinary People.* Boston: Harvard Business School Press, 2000.

Osif, Bonnie Anne. "Evaluation and Assessment, Part One: Evaluation of Individuals." *Library Administration and Management* 16 (Winter 2002): 44–48.

———. "Evaluation and Assessment, Part Two: Evaluation of Units." *Library Administration and Management* 16 (Summer 2002): 164–67.

Paine, Lynn Sharp. "Is Ethics Good Business? [interview]." *Challenge* 46 (March/April 2003): 6–21.

Pfeffer, Jeffrey. *The Human Equation: Building Profits by Putting People First*. Boston: Harvard Business School Press, 1998.

Phipps, Shelley E. "Transforming Libraries into Learning Organizations: The Challenge for Leadership." *Journal of Library Administration* 18 (1993): 19–37.

Reese, Gregory L., and Ernestine L. Hawkins. *Stop Talking, Start Doing! Attracting People of Color to the Library Profession*. Chicago: American Library Association, 1999.

Rost, Joseph C. *Leadership for the Twenty-first Century*. Westport, CT: Greenwood Press, 1991.

Rubin, Richard. "Ethical Issues in Library Personnel Management." *Journal of Library Administration* 14 (1991): 1–16.

Scholtes, Peter R. *The Leader's Handbook: Making Things Happen, Getting Things Done*. New York: McGraw-Hill, 1998.

Seaman, Scott. "An Internal Equity Evaluation System Based on Merit Measures." *College & Research Libraries* 60 (1999): 79–89.

Senge, Peter M. *The Fifth Discipline: The Art and Practice of the Learning Organization*. New York: Doubleday—Currency Paperback. 1994.

Simmons-Welburn, Janice. *Changing Roles of Library Professionals*. ARL SPEC Kits 256. Washington, DC: Association of Research Libraries, May 2000.

———. "Using Culture as a Construct for Achieving Diversity in Human Resources Management." *Library Administration & Management* 13 (Fall 1999): 205–9.

Tennant, Roy. "The Most Important Management Decision: Hiring Library Staff for the New Millennium." *Library Journal* 123 (February 15, 1998): 102.

Thomas, David A., and Robin J. Ely. "Making Differences Matter: A New Paradigm for Managing Diversity." *Harvard Business Review* 74 (September/October 1996): 79–90.

Todaro, Julie B. "The Effective Organization in the Twenty-First Century." *Library Administration & Management* 15 (Summer 2001): 176–78.

———. "What's a New Manager to Do?" *Library Administration & Management* 15 (Fall 2001): 249–51.

Urgo, Marissa. *Developing Information Leaders: Harnessing the Talents of Generation X* . London: Bowker-Saur, 2000.

Ury, William: *Getting to No: Negotiating Your Way from Confrontation to Cooperation*. New York: Bantam Books, 1993.

Welburn, William. "Do We Really Need Cultural Diversity." *Journal of Education for Library and Information Science* 35 (Fall 1994): 328–30.

Whittington, Glenn. "Changes in Workers' Compensation Laws, 2002." *Monthly Labor Review* (January 2003): 25–29.

Wilder, Stanley. *The Age Demographics of Academic Librarians: A Profession Apart. A Report Based on Data from ARL Annual Salary Survey*. Washington, DC: Association for Research Libraries, 1995.

———. "Changing Profile of Research Library Professional Staff." *ARL: A Bimonthly Report on Research Library Issues and Actions from ARL, CNI and SPARC* 208/209 (February/April 2000): 1–5.

Wilding, Thomas. "Career and Staff Development: A Convergence." *College & Research Libraries News* 10 (November 1989): 899–902.

Wiley, Carolyn. "Reexamining Perceived Ethics Issues and the Ethics Roles Among Employment Managers." *Journal of Business Ethics* 17 (1998): 147–61.

Williams, James F., III. "Managing Diversity: Library Management in Light of the Dismantling of Affirmative Action." *Journal of Library Administration* 27 (1999): 27–48.

Winston, Mark D. "The Importance of Leadership Diversity: The Relationship Between Diversity and Organizational Success in the Academic Environment." *College and Research Libraries* 62 (November 2001): 517–26.

Woodsworth, Anne, with Ellen Detlefsen, issue eds. "Managing Human Resources in Research Libraries." *Library Trends* 41/42 (Fall 1992) 180–329.

Index

About the Editors and Contributors

Editors

Beth McNeil is Assistant Dean of Libraries at the University of Nebraska-Lincoln. She joined UNL in 1996 and became Assistant Dean in 2000. Ms. McNeil has fifteen years of experience in academic librarianship in both public and technical services. As Assistant Dean, she has direct responsibility for the overall management of technical services operations, coordinates the staff development program, coordinates library-wide statistics efforts, and manages library-wide special projects. While at UNL she has led the effort to develop and implement core competencies for the library staff and faculty and developed an incentive program for library staff. She has taught library administration for graduate students in the University of Nebraska media specialist program. Prior to her tenure at the University of Nebraska-Lincoln, she was Head of Reference Services at Bradley University in Peoria, Illinois, where she was responsible for the management and administration of the reference department, supervision and training of reference department staff, collection development, budgeting, and coordination of electronic services. Previously, she served as Serials and Collection Management Librarian at Bradley. Ms. McNeil is an active member of the American Library Association, having served on committees within LAMA and ACRL. Her research interests include patron behavior, database selection, and core competencies and their development for library staff.

Janice Simmons-Welburn is the Associate Dean of the University of Arizona Libraries. She held numerous positions at the University of Iowa, including Director for Central Public Services and Facilities, and has seven years of direct responsibility for the Libraries Human Resources Program. During her tenure at the University of Iowa she developed a comprehensive staff technology education training series, expanded the Libraries staff development program to include offerings for all levels of staff, and conducted a needs assessment to ascertain current and future developmental and training needs of staff. She taught numerous in-house workshops, including management training, customer service training, and Internet skills, and has a vast array of experience in the areas of delivery of information services and end-user training from her previous roles at the University of Iowa as Head of Reference and Coordinator for System-Wide Reference Services and Director for Human Resources and Processing Services. In her twenty-four years of experience in academic libraries, she has served as Head of Interlibrary Loan at New York University, Reference Librarian at Indiana University, Georgia Institute of Technology, and Indianapolis-Marion County Public Library, and Head of the Psychology Library at Princeton University. She is an active member of the American Library Association, having served as a committee chair and member within RASD, LAMA, and ACRL, and has also presented papers and published articles on the topics of reference services, diversity, and human resources. Ms. Simmons-Welburn serves as an adjunct faculty member for the Association of Research Libraries.

Contributors

Julie Brewer has served as Coordinator for Personnel and Staff Development at the University of Delaware Library since 1989. She has a master's of public administration degree from the University of Delaware, specializing in human resources management, and a master of arts degree in library and information studies from the University of Wisconsin-Madison. An active member of the American Library Association, Julie has also published numerous articles on the topic of residency programs and other human resource issues.

Sheila D. Creth's career in the library profession spans thirty years. Beginning in 2000, she established a consulting business, Progressive Solutions, following thirteen years as University Librarian at the University of Iowa. Prior to Iowa, she held administrative positions at the libraries of the Universities of Michigan, Connecticut, and Columbia, and for seven years held an administrative position with the Columbia University Computing Center. She is a frequent contributor to the professional literature as well as a speaker at national and international conferences. She received her bachelor of arts degree in cultural anthropology with honors from Columbia University and a master of arts in communication, focusing on organization theory and research, from the University of Connecticut.

Lila Fredenburg practiced law in the area of labor and employee relations for twenty years before obtaining her MLIS degree from the University of Illinois at Urbana-Champaign in 1998. She has managed the human resources programs for Indiana University libraries and currently at Princeton University Library. She is an active member of the American Library Association.

Luisa R. Paster has been the Staff Development Librarian at Princeton University since 1996, after sixteen years in technical services at Princeton as Head of the Romance Languages Cataloging Team and Head of the Database Management Section. She has also worked with the New Jersey Train the Trainers and the New Jersey Supervisors Training Programs. Currently she is serving on the Supervisory Skills subcommittee of the Human Resources Section of the Library Administration and Management Association (LAMA).

Laine Stambaugh has been the Director of Library Human Resources at the University of Oregon Libraries since 1988. In 2001–2002, she represented the Pacific Northwest as part of the Ad Hoc Task Force on Recruitment and Retention Issues, a subcommittee of the Personnel Administrators and Staff Development Officers Discussion Group for the Association of College & Research Libraries.

Teri R. Switzer is Assistant Director for Human Resources and Budget at the Auraria Library, serving the University of Colorado at Denver, the Metropolitan State College of Denver, and the Community College of Denver. Previously, she served as the Personnel Librarian and Interim Assistant Dean for Administrative Services at Colorado State University. She received an MLS from the University of Illinois and an MBA from Colorado State University. Terri is currently the Treasurer of the American Library Association (ALA) and a member of the ALA Executive Board. Her area of publishing is in human resources and leadership.

William C. Welburn is an Associate Professor in the School of Information Resources and Library Science at the University of Arizona. He received an MSLS from Atlanta University, and a Ph.D. in Library and Information Science from Indiana University. He has served as a librarian at Indiana University, Princeton University, William Paterson College, and the University of Iowa; has taught in programs in library and information science at Atlanta University, Rutgers University, and the University of Iowa; and acted as Assistant Dean of the University of Iowa Graduate College. His professional interests include the organization of professional work in libraries and in documenting diverse cultures and communities.

Stanley J. Wilder is the Associate Dean for River Campus Libraries, University of Rochester. Prior to his current position, he served at the Louisiana State University Libraries and at the University of Illinois at Chicago Libraries. He holds an MLS from Columbia University and an MBA from the University of Illinois at Chicago. He has many published works relating to the demographics of librarianship, including *Demographic Change in Academic Librarianship* (Association of Research Libraries, 2003).

Mark Winston is Assistant Professor at Rutgers University, School of Communication, Information, and Library Studies. His current research is in the areas of leadership, management, and diversity. He edited *Managing Multiculturalism and Diversity in the Library: Principles and Issues for Administrators* and *Leadership in the Library and Information Science Professions: Theory and Practice*. He has served as a consultant and is a member of the editorial board of *College & Research Libraries*. He and co-author Kimberly Paone received the 2003 Reference Services Press Award for their *Reference and User Services Quarterly* article on information services for young adults.